CRAFTING AND REVISING DIALOGUE

A GUIDE FOR PLAYWRIGHTS, SCREENWRITERS, AND NOVELISTS

BY ALLEN GORNEY

Published 2021 by Beating Windward Press

For contact information, please visit:
www.BeatingWindward.com

First Edition
ISBN: 978-1-940761-42-8

For my Kevin

TABLE OF CONTENTS

INTRODUCTION

What is 'good' dialogue? Ask the question of a writer, reader, movie-goer or television binge-watcher, and you'll get a bunch of different responses. They'll say good dialogue is quotable. Rapid-fire. Character-defining. Or even as one of my friends says: "Good dialogue crackles." The best answer to this question is D) all of the above. Good dialogue will do all these things. You'll remember the lines, and they'll make you quote the whole darn movie.

If you're in the film industry, you've surely heard the line, "you can make a bad film from a good script, but you can't make a good film from a bad script." In sitting through many acting classes over the years, I've seen wonderfully talented actors breathe life into scripts so effortlessly one week only to flounder the next week with a completely different script. Certainly, they're connecting to one better than the other, which might be because the former exhibits characteristics they see in themselves. But what I often see is that the dialogue in some scripts is weaker, more pedestrian, more inauthentic.

Why is this?

Actors' having trouble bringing a character to life points to a serious problem about which the screenwriter or playwright must be aware. In fact, it's a serious problem about which even a novelist must be aware. These characters will become living, breathing people. They will have backstories, hopes, dreams, dilemmas, and passions. They most certainly already have them as they traverse the writers' mind, nagging and begging for their stories to be told and dramatized. But if they have such strong voices in our heads—how can that possibly translate to an inauthentic representation of the character on the page? And why would an actor—even the best actor—have trouble breathing life into those words? Where's the disconnect?

I've written this book for that reason: discovering that disconnect and how to work past it. Sure, there have been many craft books written about crafting dialogue. Writing workshops and conferences are certainly helpful. There you'll find discussion of the purpose of dialogue, its categorization as an element of storytelling, and rather arcane discussions of dialogue as an extension or expression of character. To be fair, all of that is important when talking about dialogue. But what I haven't seen yet—perhaps shockingly—is the realization that words of dialogue are meant to be spoken. In a play, the actor will say these words aloud for the audience to hear. In a film, we'll see the actors articulating memorable phrases in a close up and cut to a hilarious reaction shot. In a novel, we'll imagine these well-described, fully-formed characters saying these words for real. We'll even imagine what their voices sound like.

This book is for writers of plays, screenplays, teleplays, novels, heck—even commercials. Anything that includes dialogue. And because the method I'll be taking to teaching you how to write and revise dialogue inextricably comes from an actor's approach to the material, I'd even say this book is also a tool for actors. Everyone who writes or speaks dialogue will get something from this book.

Playwrights—whose main task is to tell a story almost wholly dependent on dialogue as the vessel—will value the emphasis I'll be placing on the actor's role in bringing the lines to life. Screenwriters and television writers will appreciate the nuances and subtleties required for that medium. Novelists will better understand the internal approaches to character—and how dialogue's sometimes spare use is a representation of a character's being compelled to speak.

I will begin this book with the basics, the essentials of writing dialogue. I will cover techniques and exercises that will allow writers to develop their characters. This will also allow actors to understand the mindset of the writer, as well as the mindset of the character they're working on. Then, I will explore how dialogue functions in various media: Theatre, film, television, and prose. Finally, I will end the book with a few case studies: explorations of dialogue in various media, complete with various drafts and commentary on the writer's process of revision. This part is perhaps the most crucial, for it's one thing to know the fundamentals of dialogue and to write it down on the page. It's another to apply the process and understand why one line is being altered. These case studies will be invaluable to demonstrating the application of the various techniques in the book.

Many writers disagree with me on this next point—some even consider me masochistic for saying it, but here it is. I love writing dialogue. I love a memorable line, a well-timed quip, a layered turn-of-phrase. I love when dialogue has melody. I love when it shows us depth and heart. I love every moment of making a line the best possible representation of a moment.

If you come along with me on this journey, by the end, you may find you'll love it too.

PART I

CHAPTER 1

WHAT DOES DIALOGUE DO?

A big feature of this book will be the analysis of dialogue: How to do it and how it functions in the drafting process of your Work-in-Progress. I'm going to give you a taste of how it will work in this book here in this chapter so you have an idea of what we're working toward. We'll be applying these techniques as a form of "close reading," deeply examining lines of dialogue to ensure they say what we want them to say and they convey the elements of dialogue we'll be discussing in this chapter.

Before we move on, let me give you a brief breakdown of terminology. In prose (novel, short story, memoir), dialogue spoken by a character often appears in quotations. The phrase after it, often marked by something like *she said* is known as a **dialogue tag.**

Let's start by examining a famous line from a classic of the English canon.

"What does Bessie say I have done?" I asked.

This line of dialogue is the first we hear the titular Jane Eyre say in Charlotte Brönte's novel. It's a fascinating line—one that tells us a lot of information about our protagonist. For one, we're told in the three preceding paragraphs that Mrs. Reed, her resentful aunt and guardian, has kept her "at a distance" because she doesn't appear to have as child-like a demeanor as her own biological children. In fact, Mrs. Reed has tasked their maid Bessie of letting her know if Jane misbehaves again, though Mrs. Reed's response to Jane's question implies to the reader she has no intention of ever treating Jane fairly, as we see here:

> "Jane, I don't like cavillers or questioners; besides, there is something truly forbidding in a child taking up her elders in that manner. Be seated somewhere; and until you can speak pleasantly, remain silent."

These two lines of dialogue are consecutive, with no description between. What they do—so early in the novel—is establish an understanding of who Jane is, what her environment is like, and how people in her life view her. Jane's first line suggests she often finds herself in trouble in this household. It isn't enough that Mrs. Reed sees a problem with Jane, but that the blame would extend to the maid connotes the whole house is against her. Mrs. Reed's line makes plausible how she rules the house and stacks it against Jane. All this information is implied between two lines of dialogue. The tone of both lines is so vivid, adverbs and adjectives aren't even necessary in the dialogue tags, and including them might rob these lines of their effectiveness. We, the modern readers, feel sympathy for Jane, while readers of Brontë's time might have understood and empathized with her.

The opening sentence of *Jane Eyre* is one of the most famous in English literature: *There was no possibility of taking a walk that day.* Leading up to Jane's first utterance in the novel, we get a sense that her life is miserable. Her first line of dialogue confirms it. It's an earned moment for Jane. It tells us who she is: Intelligent, bold, even insolent in the best possible way. It suggests we're going to see this personality heightened later, in even more tense scenarios. In fact, it even gives us a sense that this young girl is going to be fighting against and for something her entire life.

That's what a good line of dialogue does. The more you can imply, the more you can cram into that line, the better. But what are those elements? What can we pack into our lines to make them the most effective? I have four key components of dialogue—which—the closer you can get to including all four of these in each line, the better.

1. GOOD DIALOGUE REVEALS CHARACTER

We know Jane Eyre is young, under the care of her surly, cold aunt, but we get a sense from Jane's first line of dialogue and Mrs. Reed's response that Jane resents her. We also know how Jane reacts to the limited people in her life. The ensuing lines of dialogue reveal her character—who she is. Her aspirations. Her financial situation. Her family life. Her home life. How she views the world. *Her whole entire lived history.*

You'll read that sentence repeatedly in this book. I repeat it often in my workshops and in my lectures. Everything each character says should reveal some aspect of their lived history. If you think about it, everything you say in your life at any given moment reflects some aspect of your entire lived history. Your utterances reflect your values, your needs, your dreams, your social life, your education, your sense of humor—everything. It never ceases to amaze me how we can size people up as individuals, form opinions and perceive people in certain ways based on what they say, even if it's polite conversation at the grocery story. I can't tell you how many times I've gotten into discussions about some item on that conveyor belt that the clerk found interesting. Even small talk reflects some aspect of a person's lived history. That swear word you uttered at someone while driving? Again, totally reflective of who you are as a person in that moment. Maybe you despise people who don't turn on their blinkers when they intend to change lanes. That can say a lot about you. Does that set you off? Is it the little things that set you off?

Maybe that's an aspect of a character's personality. If a guy named Philip gets cut off and has to slam on the breaks, shouting, "Jeepers Creepers!" Chances are, you've formed a judgement of him. If a character says "Jeepers Creepers" in a book as some form of expletive, we know this character doesn't swear. Perhaps this character is religious. Maybe he's devout but still quick-tempered. That's a great pairing of characteristics. Imagine that dialogue—constant restraint when the guy really just wants to let it all out at the most trivial of problems.

Because dialogue reveals character, it's wholly dependent on the biography you give the character. Thus, dialogue and character are inextricably intertwined. You can't have one without the other. Think about how each line of dialogue you've written reflects the person you're depicting.

2. GOOD DIALOGUE CARRIES CONFLICT

It's simple. Characters have goals. One character has one objective. Another character has a conflicting objective. What they say tends to be in opposition to each other. That's conflict. It's going to give your dialogue that "crackling" sensation. The tit-for-tat. The one-upmanship. Dialogue is the vessel to carry the conflict—for characters to say what's on their minds, or their decision to stay mum on something, to bury their true feelings. In a medium like a play, where dialogue is the only real tool for expression, this characteristic is essential. It's different in film and prose. Characters don't have to speak as much. In a film, we can read facial expressions better, so characters don't necessarily have to talk. In a novel, we read the internal thoughts of the characters. Its dialogue is similar to film in that the character has to have a good reason to speak. When he or she does say something—it's crucial.

Recognizing the essence of conflict is crucial to crafting effective dialogue, so naturally it's important to identify what the conflict is from the outset. What does your character want in the long term? What is their **superobjective?** A superobjective is a goal the character wants to achieve by the end of the story. Many in the publishing and entertainment industry refer to this as the character's **want.** In a film, the character's want should be something tangible. It should be something the camera can see. We either see or hear the character achieving his or her want. This can be something as simple as wanting to buy ice cream or something deeper, like an attorney winning a case.

Let's take this latter example as a case study and create a fictional character. Let's say we have a fictional attorney—her name is Molly Carpenter, Esquire (and for clarity's sake, we'll title the work-in-progress *Molly Carpenter, Esquire.* Her goal in this film is to win her case and have her client Johnny found not guilty. This superobjective is filmable because at the end of the film, we can see her either winning or losing. Also—because this objective is indeed filmable, we can call this the **external superobjective.**

Since I've labeled one the **external superobjective,** not surprisingly, there's an internal one too. The **internal superobjective** is a **need.** Generally speaking, a character needs to overcome something internally to be able to achieve that external want. This is something that is more a characteristic or a vice—perhaps a character flaw. This is where we can institute one of my favorite Greek character terms: hamartia. Hamartia is a fatal or tragic flaw, which, if not overcome, will lead to this character's demise. Now, that sounds pretty melodramatic, so let's clarify "demise." Demise can be something truly horrific for your character, or it can be that your character has not overcome his or her **internal superobjective** or **need** and therefore is ill-equipped to achieve the external superobjective, or want.

Let's go back to our attorney example. Molly has to defend her client Johnny successfully, to convince the jury to acquit him. However, in order to do that, she must overcome her alcoholism. Molly's drinking is an addiction that threatens her career and her personal life. She's unable to focus, she misses meetings, and she lacks the ability to lead her defense team. Molly is great at what she does. She's a bright mind, but she drinks to mask the pain of a messy divorce. If only she could get past the problem in her life—something she **needs** to do—she could focus enough to win her case.

When Molly recognizes she needs to overcome her vice, she'll change to make herself well enough to focus better on her case. This moment of **recognition** is also known as **anagnorisis.** Very often, the anagnorisis is paired with **peripeteia,** which is the actual **moment of change**. Generally, this paired occurrence happens right after the moment of rock bottom. In a film or any story with a three-act structure, this usually happens at the end of Act II, and Act III tends to be when the protagonist regains control with enough momentum to pull them toward achieving that external superobjective. Let's say Molly recognizes that her drinking is a problem, and let's call this her low point. This happens when her assistant takes her car keys from her and forces her to take a cab home, inside which she pukes all over the cab driver. The cab driver sues for damages, but Molly is reminded that things could've been way worse for her. Not only might she lose her job and her clients, she could have ruined her life or hurt somebody else. This low point forces a change. She stops drinking, attends AA meetings, and doubles down on her work for Johnny's case. She wins the case and achieves that external goal. The internal and the external superobjective go hand-in-hand.

The reason I'm emphasizing the internal superobjective here is because this need is often what carries the theme, which brings me to the next component of dialogue.

3. GOOD DIALOGUE CONVEYS THE THEMES

A theme is a universal statement, or message conveyed by a story. Many of my students liken themes to the story's "moral." They're not incorrect—a moral can be a theme, but it's important to point out that not all themes are morals. I often demonstrate in my workshops and classes how important themes are to articulate and to construct, because it encapsulates what you're trying to say with your story—the bigger picture. In fact, I have a little formula for it.

Theme = Topic + Statement about topic

When you hear big-name actors discussing their movies in interviews, you may hear them say generalizations like, "this film is about love." Or another: "This film is about family." They're not wrong—often these films do convey elements of these broad issues. But don't so many films convey love or trust? It's a really simplistic way to discuss a film. Though that may work for advertising the film or for appealing to a wide audience, these are too broad for a writer who is in the process of constructing characters and plots that resonate.

Ideas like "love" and "family" are **topics**. They're *part* of the construction of a theme. Start there. Then, think about what your story *says about the topic*. What statement or universal idea does your story make about the topic? Perhaps it could be "real families need not be blood related." Incidentally, this is the theme behind the entire TV series "The Golden Girls." Another TV series that articulates themes really well is "Sex and the City." Each episode is thematically structured around some love or sexual topic, and Carrie Bradshaw's voiceover articulates the central theme as she writes her column. These topics range from 'how freaky is too freaky?' to 'is there such a thing as a soulmate?' to 'did we actually find true love in high school?'

Let's go back to our fictional attorney story, the case study. Molly's *want*, her external superobjective, is to get the jury to acquit her client Johnny. But she *needs* to overcome her alcoholism, her internal superobjective. This need is what carries the theme. Let's construct that theme, starting with the topic: vices. Now, what does this story say about vices? What does Molly's journey say or represent about vices? Perhaps it's *true strength lies within* if this is something she overcomes on her own, or *true friends are there when you need them most* if she relies on the benevolence of her friends who care about her.

Themes need not be expressed as a complete sentence. For example, a theme in *Jane Eyre* is about her *overcoming the rigid social class system in England.* Another theme is expressed as a dichotomy, *love versus self-reliance.* You'll notice there are multiple themes possible in a story. There are most definitely more themes in *Jane Eyre.* In fact, there will be themes you won't even be aware of when you're writing and drafting your work. Readers will discover themes. They'll see patterns you didn't even recognize. For example, I'd read *Of Mice and Men* dozens of times before I started to realize Steinbeck uses the word "furtive" quite often. Maybe he just loved the word, but still, even if subconsciously, there's a theme in the novel about hiding things—hiding one's intentions and the problems that arise from it.

So how does theme function with dialogue? How does good dialogue carry the theme? Let's take a couple of lines of dialogue from Chapter 2 of *Jane Eyre*:

> "Hold her arms, Miss Abbot: she's like a mad cat."
> "For shame! For shame!" cried the lady's maid. "What shocking conduct, Miss Eyre, to strike a young gentleman, your benefactress's son! Your young master."
> "Master! How is he my master? Am I a servant?"

Here, we have an explicit mention of one of the major themes in the novel. Jane's question "Am I a servant?" is one that Brönte explores in several of the book's episodes. Jane frequently encounters this rigid class structure and comes to know she's on the lower end. Indeed, later, as she's employed as a governess for Mr. Rochester, she again is referred to as the "help" or the lower class, despite her intellect and his growing fondness for her.

Mentions of the theme need not be so explicit—this example is one that's easy to point out. Let's take another example of theme in dialogue, using our example of Molly, the attorney. In this scene, Molly is at her lowest point, and she sits in her car outside the liquor store.

She calls her friend Kelly, and for a more dramatic depiction, let's add the pouring rain outside.

> Molly: Remember when we were in law school? It was so much easier to dream about big things. And then reality bitch-slaps you.
> Kelly: Where are you?
> Molly: It's not important.
> Kelly: Don't, okay? I can guess where you are. Don't go in there.
> Molly: It's not worth it. I'm going to lose.
> Kelly: Yeah. You got that right. You're going to lose if you go in there. But listen, you can do what you want to do. Anyway, I'm glad you called. You're the smartest litigator I know, and I really need you to help me with some evidence.
> Molly: You want my help?
> Kelly: Of course. Now how soon can you get here?

In this scene, we have Kelly imply to Molly that she needs help. She turns the tables on Molly so Molly has to leave the liquor store to help her. This implies that *true friends are there for you when you need them most*. It's not directly stated, but this is also a confidence-booster that sends the message to Molly that she's good enough at her job to help Kelly. If the scene were to continue, likely I'd end the scene on Kelly's line and cut to Kelly's opening the door to her apartment with a rain-soaked Molly smiling on her porch.

4. GOOD DIALOGUE FORESHADOWS EVENTS

Foreshadowing is a hint at future events in a story. It can be accomplished symbolically, like with a color—perhaps the little girl in red in *Schindler's List*, whom we see as the sole bit of color in a black and white movie, only to recognize that same color later after she's been killed. Naturally, in a novel, there's ample room for foreshadowing in the descriptive passages, and in film and television, visual imagery can provide the sense of foreshadowing, like the cold breaths in *The Sixth Sense*.

Foreshadowing also can be a metaphor in dialogue. General Zaroff in Richard Connell's short story "The Most Dangerous Game" mentions that he and Sanger Rainsford will play a game of "Outdoor Chess," a metaphor for the skill needed to survive in the fatal game they are about to play.

In Chapter 3 of *Jane Eyre*, Mr. Lloyd asks how much she likes her living situation at Gateshead, to which Jane replies she "should be glad to leave it." But Jane complains of not having any money, and the thought of becoming impoverished in the form of a beggar remains unappealing. She responds that she "might have some poor, low relations called Eyre." Later, as an adult, Jane learns this to be partially true. Jane does have some relations called Eyre, but her uncle was not poor. She receives a large inheritance.

How would you notice this exchange as having foreshadowing upon a first read of this novel—or any novel for that matter? The simple fact is that you don't, at least not often. You might suspect something is foreshadowing, but you'll never know if something will pay off until the story's inevitable conclusion.

Sometimes, it's a bit more glaringly obvious. Later, when Jane arrives at Thornfield, Mr. Rochester's estate, Mrs. Fairfax asks:

"How do you like Thornfield?" I told her I liked it very much.

"Yes," she said, "it is a pretty place; but I fear it will be getting out of order, unless Mr. Rochester should take it into his head to come and reside here permanently; or, at least, visit it rather oftener; great houses and fine grounds require the presence of the proprietor."

This exchange suggest that things "will be getting out of order" soon, which of course, is an understatement. In the context of the conversation, it seems like Mrs. Fairfax suggests oversight is needed, but the statement about order feels more deliberate, and even upon a first read, implies imminent conflict.

Let's go back to our attorney story and see if we can add in some foreshadowing. Suppose Molly and her friend Kelly sit out on the patio early in the script, sipping wine.

> Molly: I love that smell. The smell right before it rains. Like nature's pheromones.
> Kelly: Yeah, it was always your cue to open the windows in our dorm room. Five minutes later and we'd have to dam the waterfall dripping from the ledge.

Here, we have a seemingly innocuous conversation about rain that foreshadows Molly's rock-bottom moment later in the script. It's subtle—perhaps something that we don't notice right away, but that becomes important later. Rain is a fairly universal symbol for trouble, conflict, sadness, angst—even rebirth. So it's fitting here and says a lot about Molly as a person.

Sometimes when we reread or rewatch a book, film, or show, we pick up on these subtle instances and feel like the experience of engaging with this story is more fruitful.

Good dialogue will have these four features: conflict, character, theme, and foreshadowing. But here's the important takeaway from this chapter: it's virtually impossible to cram them all into your writing on a first draft, or even a second. Good dialogue comes from crafting and refining your characters' goals and your story's trajectory. Don't fret about the lines on those first drafts. Don't even worry about how to maximize those character profiles yet. Certainly, you'll have sketches of who these people are, but your characters are fluid until the act of writing is complete. That means your dialogue is fluid too.

EXERCISE #1

Jot down what your characters' goals are. Articulate your protagonist's external superobjective. What does your protagonist want over the duration of the novel or script? Remember that this should be something tangible—something we can see or hear the protagonist achieve at the end. Certainly, the more abstract goal of an improved self-understanding is something we see in novels, but for the purposes of this exercise, try to separate the external from the internal. So, identify that external goal. Then, think about what your character might need to overcome or to understand better in order to achieve that external goal. Do they have a flaw of some kind, or something they need to learn? That's the internal goal—the need. Write that internal goal down.

Then, think through what the external and internal goals are for all your major characters. Write those down too. Articulating their goals will help the dialogue revision separately. I always like to make sure these notes are short and sweet. They should fit on index cards with room to spare. I also usually post these over my desk to ensure I can see easily them during my revisions. However you work—keep these brief notes handy.

CHAPTER 2

CHARACTER PROFILES

We absolutely cannot talk about dialogue without having an entire chapter devoted to character. Remember that **everything your character says or does in your story reflects their entire lived history.** That biography can be subtly, indirectly referenced in dialogue and action, or it can be directly stated. Either way, it's there. It dictates character choices. It creates a vivid world of imagination for the reader or viewer. It gives the actor a firm road map to determine how to bring the character to life in the flesh.

I truly appreciate a richness of character, and I find that sometimes after reading a book or watching a TV show or film, I'll think about what that character is doing when they're not on screen. I start inventing side stories and subplot lines that were never in the original work. This works well for contemporary storytelling, which has moved toward embracing transmedia. Transmedia is loosely defined as additional stories and interactions with your characters across a wide variety of platforms. Perhaps a lesser character in your novel gets its own side-plot. Maybe the TV show branches off into comic books in the same universe. The Harry Potter series does this well, with its Pottermore, its prequels, and its stage play. Diana Gabaldon's *Outlander* series has a television series adaptation, and one of the supporting characters, Lord John, even has his own book series. With so many characters and so many possibilities of plot within that universe, the world-building is strong enough to support more stories. The TV show "Buffy, the Vampire Slayer" first began as a film, then was made into a TV show, and continued on with a spin-off (called "Angel") and a comic book series. If your characters are strong, they'll fit very easily into a well-built world.

But how do you create characters who are vivid enough to exist outside the confines of the screen or the page in our imaginations? Do you write a biography? Perhaps, if that suits your writing process. A character biography might be a prose imagining of the character's life, or perhaps a few specific episodes in a character's life. I'm personally not really much of a "character biography" writer. Even in acting school, I felt these exercises to be a bit forced. Contrived. As a writer, I feel the same way. Now, I'm not denigrating character biographies by any means. I know many writers, actors, and directors who sit and write paragraphs and pages of prose about their characters, some of which is so strong it can stand alone as its own work, like a bestselling tell-all memoir. It doesn't really work for me though. I did, however, find something that worked for me—a way to create a richness of character without spending an inordinate amount of time crafting a full biography when I really wanted just to dive right into the writing.

Create a character profile.

A character profile articulates the key features of who they are. Make it a bulleted list, something easy to refer back to. Sure, you can have multiple descriptions, even several sentences for each bullet point, but it keeps your characters' key features organized in a way that enables you to refer back to them easily.

To create a character profile, you'll need to focus on the key traits. These traits can be found under the three families of the character breakdown. They're the **physiological, psychological, and sociological** profiles of your characters, and within each of these three groups are several bullet points for which you'll create some notes.

Keep in mind that when you're defining your characters based on these traits, you're very likely not going to use every single detail. For example, with the many physiological traits of a character, if you're writing a screenplay, you really only get one sentence to describe your character in the action lines, so extraneous detail will actually work against you. And when you're writing a novel, getting bogged down with too much description and not enough action in the prose gives the reader a sense of inertia that could bore them too quickly.

What you're actually doing is creating a fully formed character that exists in your mind. You're working out the details and the subtleties of their biography that *inform* your dialogue choices. These profiles will set up guidelines for your characters, giving them consistency and focusing the subtext to reflect *their* lived histories. This will also serve as a strong index for you to go back and look at what you've written in these profiles as you revise and scrutinize every detail, every sentence, every word.

That brings me to my next point: writing dialogue is a circular process. You'll write one line. Sit on it. Hear it read aloud. Realize it doesn't work. Cross it out and start over. You'll have a turn-of-phrase in a script you think is witty only to have an actor stumble on the delivery because it actually sounds clunky. You'll write a few lines of dialogue in a novel after well-wrought prose only to find the dialogue doesn't reflect any of the character traits you created for them in their profiles. That's all okay. Keep in mind that these character profiles are fluid. They're going to change as often as you change a word. Your character details are going to change with every revision. The character attributes you gave to one character may completely swap with another character because the writing steered you in that direction.

Trust the writing. Trust yourself. Trust the characters you're birthing. They're going to guide you in the direction that's needed. As your characters change, continue changing the profiles alongside it to reflect. In the age of computers, this can be done quite quickly. I personally like to print out my character profiles and have a hard copy nearby as I write for easy reference. However, as I write, I do go back in and change the profile bullet points to reflect the changes I've made to the character in the prose. This constant record helps me stay consistent, especially if I'm dealing with a lot of detail, like when writing a novel. I'll sometimes forget who had the blue eyes, who had the brown eyes, and who was from Texas. All that will be in the easy-to-read bullet points of these character profiles. So let's get started.

1. PHYSIOLOGICAL PROFILE

Gender – Where on the gender spectrum does this character identify? Is this character cisgender male or female? Gender non-binary? Transgender? Intersex?

Age – How old is this character? In screenplays and stage plays, writers tend to give age ranges, but picking a number really helps you focus your character. I encourage you to give each character a specific age. Go as far as giving them a birthday and a zodiac sign. Even if you don't believe in astrology, zodiac signs can be fun to play with and easy to assign the more traditional traits of a sign to your characters.

Height, Weight, and Proportions – How tall is this person? How much do they weigh? What are their proportions? This may not be something that comes up in dialogue, but it certainly affects how somebody sees the world and how the world sees that person. If the character is someone who has lost two hundred pounds, she may feel like she has got a new lease on life and behaves and speaks in that manner.

Posture – Does this character slouch? Is the slouching perhaps because the character is abnormally tall? Does this character have a dancer-build with excellent posture? Again, this isn't something huge, but having an answer to this question adds layers to the character and gives you a better sense of this character's stature.

Hair, Eyes, Skin Color, and Texture – All of these deal specifically with the character's physical appearance. When I'm writing a novel with multiple characters, I find myself double-checking this bullet point the most. What was that hairstyle she was wearing? What color were his eyes? This is also where you'd include details about the character's race and ethnic background. Perhaps the character is mixed-race. What traits do they have?

Aesthetic Appearance – This detail is more a judgment call. Is this character perceived as pretty? Unattractive? You could even go as far as giving them a number—10 being model-perfect and 1 being less desirable. I've read about social experiments that demonstrated people tend to want to marry someone who is close to their own number, assuming there are no other social or monetary factors involved. If your character is married, did they marry up or down? It may sound like a demeaning thing to do, but it's something that works to give your character more of a sense of identity.

Birth Defects or Hereditary Traits – Does this character have any traits that are biologically earned? Are there some defects or inherited traits? Perhaps this character was born with profound hearing loss and now wears a cochlear implant.

2. PSYCHOLOGICAL

Sex Life – How often does this character have sex? Is he or she in a relationship? Have they hit a marital dry spell where they haven't had sex in months? Is your character a virgin? Asexual? Bisexual? Gay? Straight? Swingers? Are they in a triad? You can even go into fetishes with this bullet point. Certainly a character who is a closet-dominatrix or someone who has a foot fetish has some interesting quirks and qualities that are worth exploring.

Morality – If your character is a virgin, is it because he or she is waiting until marriage, as required by several religious? Are they devout? Even more important—do they derive their sense of morality from their religious beliefs? Do they purposely rebel against the stringent dogma in which they were raised—but are really good at heart? Are they ethical? Humane? Hypocritical in their belief system?

Level of Ambition – Is your character a go-getter? A procrastinator? Someone who can't focus on any one thing at any time? Are they a Type-A personality, someone who is competitive, controlling—a workaholic? Or are they more Type-B, less-stressed, more relaxed. Perhaps you assign your characters one of the Myers-Briggs personality traits.

Temperament – How patient is your character? Does he or she have respect for authority? Do they get incensed at someone who challenges them?

Attitude Toward Life – Is your character optimistic or pessimistic? How do they see the world? Are they introverted? Extroverted? Or do they have qualities of both—an introverted extrovert?

Neurodiversity – Does this character have some degree of neurodivergence? Do they have something going on neurologically that sets them apart? For example, is this character on the autism spectrum? Developmentally challenged? Learning disabled? Perhaps they have some form of a psychological complex. Psychological complexes can be fun to play with and can add a nice dimension to your characters, particularly the villains. Most villains operate from a specific pathology, and this is where you define what that is. Perhaps your character does have some form of complex, but it *doesn't* make them the villain. Does your character have Narcissistic Personality Disorder? A Napoleon Complex? Adonis Complex? Barbie Complex? Are they severely depressed? Are they abusive? Victims of abuse? Do they have a complex about that? Are they a sociopath? Do they have Delusions of Grandeur? All of these are potential aspects of this characteristic.

Talents – Maybe your character has a very specific talent. Can they sing? Dance? Play a musical instrument? Are they great at sports? Are they fast runners? Maybe they're hyper-flexible. Maybe they're telepathic. They can cast spells. Do magic. Time travel.

Qualities – This is where you give the character some specific adjectives, and I find that this bullet point is one that sticks to my characters the most. I generally assign the character two or three qualities and let that guide me in their construction. These characteristics usually have one that seems contradictory, which has the added bonus of allowing my characters to grow as round as possible—for them to feel completely whole and real. Perhaps the character is sarcastic and witty but has a heart of gold. Maybe the character is ambitious and a dreamer but uncommunicative. I like to print these qualities onto index cards and tack them over my desk so I'm constantly reminded of them when I'm drafting. Again, these qualities can change over the many revisions, but it's nice to have a place to start.

IQ – Assign a number. Is your character a genius? That would be an IQ of over 140. Are they in Mensa? Are they a savant? Are they gifted, IQ of 125-134? Or Above Average, 115-124? Are they on the severe low end, 50-70 or even lower? Do some research on what these qualities might entail and give your character a number. What's even more important of a question to consider here is *to what extent does your character let this number define who they are?*

3. SOCIOLOGICAL

Class – Social class is important to determine for your characters, mostly because it's a foundational representation of a person's sociological profile. Note that social class is not necessarily always tied to the education level of a character; you can have very wealthy, upper-class people with little-to-no education beyond high school. Maybe your character has an eighth grade education but won the lottery. Especially in a period piece, social class is crucial to define, for it will define the very existence of your characters. Most Ancient Greek stories are stories of the wealthy: citizens who owned slaves, land, and held a position of prominence. We may read stories of the same scenarios from the slave's point of view, but that slave is still a part of that class system. The only other Greek stories we hear about are those of soldiers in the military. Rare is the story of the low-class free man in Ancient Greece, or the homeless free man.

Jane Eyre's major predicament is that she's considered low-born. She has few prospects, and when she does earn money, it's as a governess to the ward of a wealthy man. This situation is so crucial to the plot and her characterization that it's a major part of her growth. Therefore, her ability to find a sense of identity in this world is wholly dependent on where she works and for whom. The bottom line here is that you must define class for your characters, whether contemporary or historical.

Education – The character's education level is also crucial to how they speak. However, it's important to point out that it's not necessarily true that a more educated person, perhaps someone with a Phd., would not speak in slang or would not use a word like "ain't." The context, however, is important. If said Phd-holder were at an academic conference or in a more formal setting, they would tailor their words to a higher register. So, context is important. The scene and setting are important. But still, define your character's education level. Is he or she poorly-educated? Did they graduate but go to a poor school district? Did they attend a highly-competitive college? Community college? Trade school? Do they have a Bachelors degree at all? Did they start college but drop out because they found it difficult to learn in a structured environment? The more you can answer for your characters here, the better. At the very least, define the level of education they went to. I like to pick a college or university because then I can describe that character's affinity to the school, reflected in clothing. I can give them a college ring to wear. It helps to define the colors of the clothing— school colors on game day.

You may even choose to give them a major and a minor. This adds some dimension to the character because, naturally, this adds dimension to a person. Perhaps your character majored in biology and went on to medical school but minored in Spanish and therefore worked for Doctors Without Borders in a Spanish-speaking country for a time.

Occupation – What does your character do for a living? It's not always the case, but sometimes the character's college major is applicable to what they do for work. Maybe they majored in something and realized later in life that wasn't really what they wanted to do. I know many actors with degrees in accounting, engineering, sciences, business—you name it. Most often those degrees do not prepare them to be actors professionally.

Home Life – This one can apply one of two ways: If your character is an adult, this can apply to their life as someone who is of age. If that's the case, then you'll need to apply a separate, perhaps different home life situation for their childhood. This can differ vastly, and arguably, the latter case is more important. What someone's childhood life is like plays a strong factor in how they see the world later in life. What was their childhood like? Were they from a nuclear family? Divorced home? Shared custody? Was one parent absent from their life? Were they one of many siblings? In which birth order are they? The oldest child certainly has a different experience growing up than the middle or youngest child. Was this character abused as a child? How does all of that factor into the adult life? Do they carry on the same traditions they had in their childhood? Have they completely blocked out their childhood? Don't skip this step; it's an important part of the process of rounding out your character and giving them a worldview.

Religion – What is this character's religion? The answer to this question also has a bearing on the character, particularly if they were born into the religion. Chances are, they derive their sense of morality from their religion. Even if they abandoned their religious beliefs at some point, some of those beliefs may still be imprinted on how they see the world. Were they completely secular from birth? Did they marry into a religious tradition or marry someone with completely opposite beliefs? The answers to this question will closely mirror the answers to the *morality* bullet point in the psychological profile, so if there's some overlap here, that's totally okay. But think about how this character's religious life has factored into social relationships. Perhaps they were members of a church or synagogue community growing up, or maybe they're still part of one.

Place in Community – Does your character do anything for the community in which he or she lives? Is he a big man on campus? President of the Student Government Association? A community activist? Does she canvass for votes? Is she the friendly neighbor? Is he the crazy recluse with all the trees and vines around the house? More importantly, how does the community view this person? It's not uncommon now for neighbors not to know each other's names, or anything beyond a first name. Is that the case here with your character? Perhaps the walls in your character's apartment are thin, and they can hear everything said and done in the next unit—and maybe that terrifies them that someone could be listening to them. Everything with this bullet point includes how the character interacts with their community.

Assimilation – This bullet point continues with the ideas of the "place in community." To what extent is this character assimilated into the community. Is this character an outsider? Is there a language barrier? Does this character feel like he or she "belongs" to the community—or better yet, *a* community. Remember that communities don't just have to be centered on the physical neighborhood in which the character resides. A community can be a group of people who come together for a sense of togetherness and/or a specific purpose. Generally speaking, however, an individual who joins a group specifically is someone who has sought out that group. But society does group people together by identity. For example, perhaps your character is gay and therefore defaults, according to society, to the "gay community." But maybe this character feels ostracized by the gay community, or shuns the label. Think about how much your character identifies with the community around them, both physical and abstract.

Political Affiliation – Is your character politically active? Do they vote? Do they live in a society where there is voting? Think about the world of your character. Are there political factions? Is it a monarchy or a dictatorship, and any political opposition is illegal? What are the rules in that world, and where does your character lie on the political spectrum? If your character doesn't even think about politics, why? Are they a Democrat, Republican, or Independent? Consider that many countries have their own political parties. For example, a Republican in the United States might be a Tory in the United Kingdom. A Republican in Ireland means something completely different. Since politics is an ever-shifting, ever-evolving part of a person's identity, determining to what extent your character adheres to the platform of a political party is important. The more detail you can give here the better.

Hobbies – In what extracurricular activities does your character participate? Since this is under the sociological profile, think in terms of what activities your character does that requires him or her to be around others. This is closely related to their talent, but whereas talent is mostly an individual trait, hobbies can include pastimes that involve other people. Is your character a member of a knitting circle? Does she play a team sport? Are they a member of a running club? Note that these groups differ from "support groups," since the hobby needs to demonstrate that the individual uses his ability as the basis for joining this group.

EXERCISE #2

Complete the character profile for each major character in your work. However you define "major character" is up to you, but you should have a full biography or bulleted list of these categories for each character. Remember this process is fluid; what you write here can and will change as your work-in-progress grows and deepens. Don't let these bullet points be shackles or hard rules for your characters. Trust that the trajectory of your story may change, and as such, these bullet points will change. Update them as this happens.

CHAPTER 3

WRITING DRAMATIC DIALOGUE

I hesitated naming this chapter "Dramatic Dialogue" because it sounds a bit pompous. In fact, the original title for this chapter was "Writing Realistic Dialogue." But that was completely contrary to the point of this chapter. Dialogue shouldn't be "realistic" or "natural"; it should be *dramatic*. Now, I'm not talking melodramatic, as if some deep-voiced baritone actor speaking with an affectation were to deliver it. I'm talking about dialogue that is heightened to the circumstances in your work. Dull dialogue is indeed natural dialogue. Daily, I engage in small talk with people at work, people at the store, people everywhere I go. It might sound something like this:

> Him: Hi, How are you?
> Me: I'm doing well. How are you?
> Him: Good. Glad I beat the rain.
> Me: Yeah. Looks like it's gonna start pouring.

This exchange is something you might encounter every day, but it doesn't really go anywhere. It's *natural* and *realistic*, but it's—to use a contemporary idiom—basic. Now, I know what you're thinking. In my example from the previous chapter, I used rain in the dialogue as foreshadowing in this exchange:

> Molly: I love that smell. The smell right before it rains. Like nature's pheromones.
> Kelly: Yeah, it was your cue to open the windows in our dorm room. Five minutes later and we'd have to dam the waterfall dripping from the ledge.

Sure, they're talking about rain, and rain is dull. But there's more depth here than in the aforementioned exchange between *me* and *him*. For starters, we get a glimpse of Molly as a character. She's somewhat poetic, and she loves something that's a bit more unconventional that might just say something about her mental state and her inner workings. We also get a little more detail about Kelly. We know they were dorm roommates in college, and we understand that she knows Molly pretty well. The exchange between Molly and Kelly is more dramatic in the sense that we discover more about them. In the exchange between *me* and *him*, we learn nothing new about the characters.

I'm not big on those pleasantries. The "hello, how are you?" exchanges are mostly pointless, and too much of it sounds false. If you don't believe me, watch Tommy Wiseau's cult film *The Room*. That's a film with an abundance of pleasantries so egregious, you come to appreciate how awkward they sound. As a general rule, the only time pleasantries are acceptable are if a) you're writing a period piece, and there's a historical greeting you need to include, and even then it really should only be done if you have b) a character's name to introduce. The first time the audience sees a character, it's generally important to get their name. That's where a pleasantry can come in handy. But rest assured, a more creative workaround is needed. This is especially the case among writers of short screenplays and short stories. I'm already big on economizing dialogue as much as possible, but in a short work, you have even less space to convey character, so character introductions should be creative and should *imply* a relationship.

For example, let's take a look at our *Molly Carpenter, Esquire* story, with an introduction to both Molly and a senior partner at her firm that could use some work. She's an associate attorney, and she's been running late for a meeting with a senior partner at her firm. She bursts into the meeting room panting, hoisting her briefcase up to the conference table before taking her seat.

> Molly: Hi, Brad. I'm sorry I'm late. The dog needed walking and then there was an accident on the highway. The traffic was awful. I hit every light. I hope I didn't miss too much. I'm all ears.
> Brad: Molly, this is a constant problem. You're always late and you always have the same excuse.

The first draft of this conversation isn't awful. It reveals a little bit of character, but it's wordy, clunky, and not a great way to maximize character in a short span of time. A screenplay or a stage play doesn't give us a whole lot of time to develop characterization, so we really need to economize as much as possible. Let's take a look at the same conversation, only this time, let's reduce the word count significantly.

> Molly: Sorry, Brad. It—
> Brad: Traffic again?

Here, instead of her walking in and beginning with a pleasantry, she cuts right to the apology *and* tells the audience Brad's name for the first time. Moreover, Brad's response tells us Molly is habitually late. The curt response also implies he's not pleased with her constant tardiness. We get a good sense of Molly and Brad's relationship here in so few words. Brad believes she's unreliable and always has excuses.

Molly also implies that she knows this is a problem and was going to rely on another excuse.

You'll notice in each of these exchanges that the dialogue is written in sentence fragments. This is perhaps why so many writing gurus say dialogue should be realistic or should sound natural. People speak in sentence fragments and rarely speak in complete sentences. It's not something that's an indication of class or education level. It's a simple fact of communication. People are going to say what they need to say in the most economical way possible.

In our everyday lives, we abbreviate. We shorten. We use metonymy—a word or substitution representing the thing its meant to define. For example, "The White House issued a proclamation today." *White House* here stands for the President or the Executive Branch of the United States Government. When I taught high school English, my students referred to my class by my last name. They'd say, "Did we have any homework in Gorney?" Naturally, the full intended sentence was "Did we have any homework in Mr. Gorney's class?" Still, the shortened version was intelligible by all of my students.

I'm a big advocate for proper grammar, but dialogue grammar gets a pass. Your characters will speak in metonymy. They'll speak in fragments. They'll have one-word answers. You'll invent marvelous shorthand for them, as in the film *Clueless*, in which screenwriter Amy Heckerling creates slang for her characters that's so darn catchy it actually worked its way into the real slang of that generation. And everyone knows Tina Fey's *Mean Girls* joke about making fetch happen.

That's not to say grammar doesn't have its place, but my adage is **clarity trumps everything.** Your lines, above all else, need to be clear. For example:

Take your hands off Molly.
Take your hands off, Molly.

One blames Molly. The other does not. The comma for direct address happens to be my biggest pet peeve comma error. You'll need to obey *those* rules when writing dialogue. But you can have… er… you can put in… all kinds of pauses and even—

Cut people off.

Good dialogue is going to have sentence fragments. It's going to emphasize specific words, even naturally. It's going to use repetition in a way that's interesting and dynamic. In fact, the more grammatical variety you can put into your writing, the better. The more rhetorical devices you can play with to reveal character, the better. Make it a life-long goal to study rhetoric. Devices are fantastic when used judiciously and purposefully. In the Part II of this book, I have a list of some of my favorite devices to use to give the dialogue a little more flare. Use sparingly, and consider what they add to your characters as a deliberate choice.

Although dialogue is supposed to be dramatic as opposed to realistic or naturalistic, it's great to get a sense of how people speak. Outside London stands Hampton Court Palace, one of King Henry VIII's many palaces, but one of the few that has been preserved. In the Great Hall, if you look up in the beams, you'll see carved figurines peering over the eaves. These literal "eavesdroppers" were supposed to remind the courtiers that someone was always listening to the secrets and the gossip.

That's what you're going to do for the exercise in this chapter. You're going to listen.

EXERCISE #3

Go to a restaurant or a public park and eavesdrop on a conversation. Without any context, see if you can figure out what the subject is. It's fascinating how you can pick up on clues, tone, and sentence structure to determine a lot about the people talking. I do this all the time. It doesn't mean I'm nosy (okay, maybe it does), but I like to think of it as research. Sometimes, I'll overhear one side of a telephone conversation and try to fill in the other side in my mind. This is great practice for two reasons. 1) you're getting a nice variety of speech patterns and 2) you're getting a good sense of the subtleties of dialogue.

The subtleties of dialogue are crucial here, and it's a great place to leave off this chapter. Dialogue does not need to *tell* us everything. Dialogue can *imply* things. Using this Eavesdropping exercise, we get a sense of who the speakers are and the situation without a direct statement of the context. We don't need to be told everything to read between the lines. That makes for the best, most compelling dialogue.

CHAPTER 4

DRAFTING THE FIRST DRAFT

hope you noticed that I'm referring to the first draft with a number. I don't like the term "rough draft." Calling it that belies so much of the writing process because it implies there will only be one draft and it will be rough. However, I will acquiesce the word "rough" is probably accurate; there is nothing polished about the first thing you churn out after laboring in front of the screen for hours, days, months, perhaps even years, trying to get the thoughts on the page. But there will be many drafts—dozens of drafts even.

But of course, it starts with that first draft. Before I give you my advice for writing that first draft, it's worth it to define the type of writer that you are. Are you a **pantser** or are you a **plotter**? A **pantser** is someone who writes *by the seat of their pants*. With little planning and no outline, these writers dive in and let the story unfold, discovering character, voice, plot—everything—along the way. This approach always fascinates me because, if you haven't guessed by the first three chapters of this book, I'm the total opposite. So, my suggestion to pantsers is to at least think through the character profiles and your characters' superobjectives. Let them marinate. Then, dive in and swim, spelunking through the intricate caverns and winding paths of your subterranean wonderland. I will always be in awe of you.

If you are a **plotter**, that means you plan. If you're like me, you outline the whole story, and perhaps write a **treatment**, a prose summary of the entire plot. You may write character biographies beforehand, or you may choose to use bulleted lists for your character profiles. Then, you write that first draft, knowing which direction the story is going, but always staying open to new discoveries and potential changes along the way.

Whether you're a pantser or a plotter, the bottom line is to get that first draft written. Don't worry about the nuances of dialogue or style just yet. Get the plot down and allow the story to take some shape. You'll sand down those rough edges later, smoothing it all out so it can be painted with shades of meaning.

If you hit a rough patch where you feel like it's all falling apart, you're not alone. This happens to every writer. We all have our existential moments where the whole thing feels like it's not working, and where you want to give up and question all of your life's choices. Totally, perfectly normal.

Some writers like to use a daily quota. I have done this, trying to write something like 50,000 words in a prose novel or getting a 100-page first draft of a screenplay or stage play written in a month. If that works for you, do the math and determine how many words or pages you need to churn out in a day. If you have no deadline or need to impose an arbitrary number of days in which to write, simply find the best writing schedule for yourself.

I know that can be hard. With spouses, kids, pets, work responsibilities, we can be pulled in a million different directions. But carve out some "writing time," whether it's each day for a half an hour, or a longer chunk of time a few days each week. You need that time to yourself to write. If that means you need to take your laptop to someplace outside your home, do it. I sometimes find there are too many distractions at home, and I need to go somewhere to write. When I get stuck on something, I like to take a walk. Literally walk. I'm a big believer in the physical-to-mental connection. Something about being away from the computer for a little bit helps. If a walk is not an option, find something else physical you can do to get the blood flowing. It can be cleaning, or even chair yoga. Some light stretching. Then, make yourself a cup of coffee or tea and get to work.

Whatever your writing habits are, whichever approach you take, the goal is the same for everyone: get that first draft down on the page. Finish it. After that first draft and when you're ready, start putting the advice and exercises in the chapters that follow to use. Trust that at some point in a later draft, your characters will start speaking authentically, and with a strong sense of purpose. They will begin to take shape and speak with dynamic, interesting personalities.

When you're done with that first draft, take some time away for a little bit. Then return to your completed work and read it in its entirety, from start to finish, taking the whole thing in. Get a feel for the story you've written, and don't feel bad if you think it's terrible. So many writers feel that way about their first drafts. They're just the beginning. Read the pages and think about them. When you've done that, you're ready to move on.

PART II

CHAPTER 1

A NEW DIRECTION

Part Two of this book is where we get into the real meat of revising dialogue. Revision is the essential step in the process of crafting dialogue. Let's start this section by picking up where you've left off. You already have a draft of your Work-in-Progress, and you've given yourself a moment to sit down and read the text from start to finish to take in the work as a whole. Make sure you've made some general notes of your overall impression of the work now that you can see it in its entirety. Perhaps you've given your first draft to someone else to read. Look at their notes as well. Take a moment and think about the biggest notes—the notes I consider to be the House of Cards notes. These are usually big elements like plot, conflict, and theme, and without them, your whole story falls apart, like taking the bottom cards away from the tenuous structure you've created. Address those global notes first. If you're stuck, move on in this book anyway. Some of the advice in the next few chapters may clarify your process or your story more.

If you've breezed through Part One of this book because you already understand how to develop a well-rounded character and/or you have your own process for doing so, you'll be ready to put the upcoming techniques to use right away. If you struggled a bit, don't worry. The next few chapters may help you clarify your story.

CHAPTER 2

THE CHARACTER'S EXTERNAL SUPEROBJECTIVE

As mentioned earlier in this book, the character's external superobjective is the character's long-term "want." Over the course of the story, the character is trying to achieve this objective. Since this is external, the character's want should be something tangible. This is something we can see or hear the character achieving by the end of the story. In film, this is important since it helps the audience root for that specific character to be successful on his or her journey. Let's look at a few examples.

In *The Wizard of Oz* (film) and *The Wonderful Wizard of Oz* (novel), Dorothy's external superobjective is clearly stated: She wants to get home to Kansas. This want can be summarized in the **central dramatic question**. A central dramatic question is a direct question that states the overarching conflict—the journey—of every character. It should be stated as **will character (action verb) (object)**? For *The Wizard of Oz*, the question is *Will Dorothy return home?* This is her goal throughout the whole film, and she famously states that "there's no place like home."

In the book *Crafting the Character Arc* by writing structure guru Jennie Jarvis, she explains that the *Lord of the Rings* trilogy also has an external superobjective. Now, I know what you're thinking—the obvious answer here is that Frodo's goal is to destroy the ring. As Jennie explains in her book, that's partially true, and you wouldn't be entirely wrong if that was your immediate thought. But think about why it is Frodo needs to destroy the ring. He needs to save the Shire—his home. That's been the task thrust upon him. His duty and responsibility is to embark on the journey to Mordor to cast the ring into its fires, but the *reason* he goes is to save the Shire.

In Jameson Tabard's darkly comedic novel *The Scottish Bitch*, a modern update of William Shakespeare's *Macbeth* with drag queens, protagonist Latrine Dion, who assumes the dramatic function of the original titular Macbeth, wants to win the title of Grand Dame in a competition of the same name. To do so, she has to win the regional Duchess competition, and following a similar plot of Macbeth, she takes out her competition in fabulously dark ways. Therefore, the central dramatic question can be expressed here as *Will Latrine win the Grand Dame Competition?*

In Disney's *Coco*, twelve-year-old Miguel dreams of playing his guitar in the plaza as a musician, but after he steals the guitar of the legendary and now-deceased musical superstar Ernesto de la Cruz, he is transported to the Land of the Dead. At that point, his goal morphs into something even more tangible and immediate—he must return to the Land of the Living or he will be stuck permanently among the dead—as one of them. The goalposts move a few times because as he's stuck in the Land of the Dead, he must receive a blessing from his great-great grandmother Imelda, who will only grant it if he gives up his dream of being a musician. But he still wants to become a musician. Therefore, *Will Miguel become a musician?* is his true central dramatic question, despite his having to return home to the Land of the Living.

Certainly, with all of these examples, there are deeper circumstances with these characters. A greater sense of *why* these external goals are so important and so meaningful becomes important. That's coming up in the next chapter—where we discuss that internal need that fuels the external goal. You surely also have noticed that in each of these examples, the characters all stand to lose something significant if they do not achieve their goals. That's important—the stakes are high, and that keeps the audience invested in this journey.

TELEVISION

A quick note on goals for television shows. There are two types of television series: The serial and the episodic. In a serial, the goal continues on over the course of the season, if not the entire series. In a show like Netflix's *Ozark*, protagonist Marty Byrde must heal the rift he created with a dangerous drug cartel by moving to the Ozarks and setting up a money laundering operation. That plotline carries over multiple episodes and multiple seasons. In a show like *Law and Order*, though there are consistent characters, each episode generally deals with solving a specific crime within the single episode. Occasionally, the crime will cover a two-parter, two episodes devoted to solving that crime. Some shows have become known for blending these two types together. *How to Get Away With Murder* has a longer, more serialized storyline that can extend over the season, and each episode in Seasons two and three deal with that storyline in addition to a new defendant Annalise Keating's firm must defend.

You may find that, after you've read your first draft, your protagonist's external superobjective isn't strong enough to sustain three full acts in a screenplay or get you to the final chapters of your novel. If you find your characters running out of steam, **raise the stakes.** When you raise the stakes, your characters stand to lose more if they do not achieve their objectives. Raising the stakes makes that goal more personal to the character; it makes them want to fight harder for it. You can also add more obstacles to make the character's external superobjective that much harder to achieve.

OBJECTIVES ON A SMALLER SCALE

Now that we have discussed the importance of the external superobjective, a goal the character has over the duration of the work, we should move on to the scene objectives. **Scene objectives** are more immediate, and they're really the lifeblood of writing effective dialogue. A scene objective is a short-term goal your character wants to achieve within the context of a scene or a sequence. In a novel, this objective may take place over the course of a chapter or a section, or even a few chapters. In any medium, the scene objective for your character should connect, to some extent, to your character's larger external superobjective.

Let's take our attorney story *Molly MacDonald, Esquire*. Molly's external superobjective is to win her case; that stretches across the entire narrative. In one particular scene, Molly has to convince her assistant to work overtime. This scene objective connects to the larger goal of winning her case, but it's smaller scale here. Moreover, the stakes are high. Molly wants to win her case, but the immediate goal is to convince her assistant to help her prepare questions for a witness. The assistant—let's call him William—has plans to go out with his buddies for happy hour. It's not a particularly strong goal for Will. He doesn't stand to lose much if he doesn't achieve his goal, so let's raise the stakes for him. Let's say that if Will does not achieve his objective of leaving for happy hour, he won't see the friend he hasn't seen in two years who flew into town for the weekend.

Now, Molly has to work hard to convince Will to stay. This conversation can turn into a negotiation of sorts, which is what I envision for it. Let's see what this looks like with strong goals:

Molly: Where are you going?
Will: It's 5:00, Ms. Carpenter. Wherever I want.
Molly: Any chance I can convince you to stay?
Will: Not really.

Molly: I need you to stay.

Will: From nine to five each day, with the exception of my lunch break, you get to tell me what to do. After that, you're on my time.

Molly: I know it seems like I've been really stressed out lately, and I know I've been taking it out on people, but...

Will: It's now 5:01. You can tell me about your stresses in the morning if you'd like. Until then, have a good night.

Molly: Wait.

Will stops.

Molly: I'm willing to pay you overtime.

Will: That you want to pay me overtime tells me you're not looking for just an hour more of work. So again, I'll see you tomorrow.

Molly: Double time. I'll pay you double time.

Will: You don't get it. I have plans, Molly. It's Friday. Contrary to how I might make it seem, I don't live to work here.

Molly: I'm sorry for treating you like garbage.

Will: Okay, that's a start. I'm kind of—.

Molly: Surprised. I know. It's a new leaf.

Will: You really need me to stay.

Molly: I do.

Will: Why all of a sudden do you trust my judgment and work ethic enough to want me to stay?

Molly: I always have. I know I have a funny way of showing it.

Will: Funny is what you're calling it.

Molly: Not funny, but... you know what I mean.

Will: Double time is still on the table.

Molly: It is.

Will: Okay, let me text my buddies I'll be two hours late. I'll owe them a full round of drinks now, and not at the happy hour price.

Molly: Two hours? What if I need you to stay longer?

Will: Two hours, Ms. Carpenter.

Molly: Right. And you can call me Molly even though you're on the clock.

Will: Two hours starts now.

In this scene, Molly's objective is to get Will to stay and help her. If she does not achieve this goal, she stands to lose the opportunity for help from someone she knows will work hard and cut her labor in half. Her goal pretty consistently stays the same across the entire scene; her tactics change a couple of times from *inquire* to *plead* to *negotiate* to *apologize* to *praise* and back to *negotiate*, all in an effort to keep Will there.

However, Will's goal does fluctuate. His goal starts out as leaving the office. Then it becomes to get Molly to see that she's been difficult to work for. Then it becomes laying out the terms of his staying late. It's perfectly acceptable for a character's goal to change over the course of the scene. In fact, it demonstrates that your character is using various tactics to get what he or she wants. Moreover, sometimes obstacles arise mid-scene, and your character's new goal is to get past the obstacle. I call these changes in tactic **action beats.** Action beats are the duration of a specific tactic the character will use to achieve his or her objective in the scene. When the tactic changes, I call that a **beat change.** These are different from emotional beats or "beats" in the theatrical sense of "pauses." I actually prefer to view these action beats as more important because they remind us as writers that the actor will be *doing* something in the scene to achieve his or her goal.

Let's look at where these beats are in the scene for Will. In the aforementioned paragraph, I stated Will's goal was to leave the office. Though I have not included much blocking (the character's movement and activity in the scene), I can see him closing his computer, putting on his coat, and slinging his messenger bag over his shoulder. That blocking is a visual cue to Molly as much as it is to the audience, whether this is a play, novel, or film. Will maintains this goal for handful of lines.

Here's where we get into the nitty-gritty of making dialogue as strong as possible. Don't view these lines as a means to tell the story. **View these lines as a tactic.** They're action. They're a means for Will to get what he wants. An obstacle has been thrown his way in the form of Molly's catching him, but his goal of leaving the office still remains. Examine each line in this section and determine what it is Will is *trying to do with that line.* Again—he's trying to leave. You could even say he *wants to tell Molly he's leaving.* That brings an interesting connotation in that he feels compelled to tell her what he's doing. Sure, she's his boss and it's a professional courtesy, but if he really believes what he's saying—that she has no say in what he does after five o'clock—then it doesn't really matter. Then, distill each tactic down to a simple action verb to the best of your ability.

The use of the action verb in this exercise is key in that you're cognizant of the tactic the actor would use. Even if you're a novelist, imagine an actor would be saying your lines. These actions help to keep your dialogue tight and conflict-laden. You will do this for each character in the scene. Because we have two characters here, it's easier to see that Molly and Will have conflicting goals. That works well because it heightens the tension and the drama in the scene. Molly's tactic is to convince Will to stay. Her action verb is *convince.* Will's action is to *avoid.*

Note that these action verbs must be transitive. A transitive verb is a verb that requires a direct object. For example, Will's goal is to *avoid Molly.* Molly is the direct object in that sentence. Molly's goal is to *convince Will.* Will is the direct object in that sentence. This distinction is important because the action must be *done to* someone or something in the scene. That keeps the action as tangible as possible. An *intransitive verb*—a verb that does not have a direct object—is ineffective for this exercise. For example, in the sentence *Molly grows up,* "grows up" is the verb phrase, but it does not require a direct object. Certainly there is some action to growing, but it does not immediately require someone or something in that moment. It's therefore an ineffective tactic.

Do not substitute adjectives for this exercise. I've had students and writers attempt this exercise by using a word like "anxious." Anxious is not an action; it's a state of being. It's a feeling. It describes the action rather than demonstrating it. Certainly, Will might be annoyed in this scene, but "annoyed" is not an action. Consider that he's avoiding Molly in that moment. You certainly can layer in other actions, and there's an internal objective as well. That's coming up in the next chapter.

It's certainly debatable where the action beat change is in this scene—the moment where Will changes his tactic from *avoid* to something else. A logical place where we see one is Will's first longer line: "From nine to five each day, with the exception of my lunch break, you get to tell me what to do. After that, you're on my time." Here, we see a unique perspective in that the subordinate is lecturing his boss—it's bold and though the external action verb shouldn't focus on suggesting other factors, it works well in that it implies a pattern of behavior on Molly's part of treating Will poorly—one Will resents. Thus, *lecture* feels like an accurate verb to describe what's going on. Other verbs will work. You can probably think of three or four. But to keep this simple, let's start with the one action. As you get more into the process, you can add a secondary, but keep in mind that these are external, tangible actions that can be done to the other person.

Will's tactic of *lecturing* carries on for a few lines before Molly utters her apology: "I'm sorry for treating you like garbage." Molly cuts right to the chase here. She owns her behavior. We believe she's sincere because *Will* believes she's sincere. His action verb continues in this direction, even through Molly's line. When she's finished speaking, his response of "Okay, that's a start. I'm kind of—." His tactic softens here to a less aggressive verb. In fact, it's one that seems to *accept* her apology and *express* his feelings about it. Those two verbs indicate the goals for the two sentences in this line. A single line of dialogue can have multiple tactic changes in it; therefore, it can have multiple action verbs to describe it. He continues with this same action for the next couple of lines.

Will's line "Why all of a sudden do you trust my judgment and work ethic enough to want me to stay?" also represents a tactic change because now it almost seems too good to be true for Will. He *questions* her intentions because he's skeptical. Here, *question* is an effective action verb that represents Will's external objective in the scene.

Now, I know what you're thinking. We haven't quite discussed Will's superobjective. He's not a major character in this story, but every character with a major speaking role should have an ultimate destination—an ultimate goal. Even if it's something that you won't use or ever mention in the narrative, giving each character a full arc will give them even more of a sense of roundness—a sense of complete characterization. You'll understand the character better and be able to make more informed choices in their dialogue. Moreover, you'll better understand their **dramatic function.** A dramatic function is the overall purpose a character serves in the story. They can function within the realm of archetypes, like the "dumb" one, the "promiscuous" one, the "type A," etc. Or, they can function as a story element that pushes the momentum forward. Sometimes a character functions as the audience's point of view. The character Jim in the television series "The Office" fits this function. He has a distinct characterization as the "normal" one in a cast of a bunch of other types. He even has a relationship to the camera that allows him to convey his unspoken feelings about specific circumstances or occurrences within the shot, marked by his glances directly into the lens.

Identifying Will's dramatic function is important here. He's going to represent the impact Molly's drinking has had on her mood and her legal practice. He's disenchanted and wants to move on. He really doesn't even care if he gets fired. So, Will's goal—his external superobjective—is to find a new job. Sure, he probably doesn't want to spend the time looking for one and would probably prefer a sincere apology instead, but in his mind, he's reached a breaking point. Again, this may be something that's never mentioned explicitly in the text, but it may be alluded to. More importantly, it helps shape the mood, tone, word choice—even syntax—of his dialogue.

Back to the script: Will's line "You really need me to stay" is a recognition line. His anagnorisis. If we're determining that Will's goal is to find a new job, this moment might change his mind. Indeed, it does. The action verb representing the tactic in this line is perhaps *verify*. You might even say it's *boast*. That could even be the subtext (more on that in the next chapter).

Another tactic change in the scene—perhaps the last—is with the line "double time is still on the table." Here, he may be negotiating, but given the tone of the next few lines and his recognition a few lines back, *dictate* is a stronger verb. He's *dictating* the terms of his staying for the evening. Will realizes he's got the upper hand. She "really needs him to stay," and he even sees that it's enough to make her apologize and demonstrate to him how she really feels about him—that she appreciates him. That's enough for him to stop looking for another job. His staying may even be trial run. We don't know for sure. We might never know that. But that little hint of possibility is great for these two characters. It shows growth for Molly and vindication for Will. And for the audience or reader—we get to have fun filling in the blanks. The characters also get to live when they're not on screen or on the page. That's when you know you have strong dialogue, and strong dialogue leads to strong character.

Let's take a look at a moment from a classic play *Mrs. Warren's Profession* by George Bernard Shaw. *Mrs. Warren's Profession* is a four-act play in which the titular character, Mrs. Warren, tries to reconcile with her daughter Vivie. Vivie has been ashamed of her mother for engaging in a profession her society deems improper: Mrs. Warren is the madam of a brothel and is herself a former prostitute. Vivie's dilemma runs deeper because although there is impropriety in Mrs. Warren's profession, she has reaped the benefits of living a comfortable lifestyle, one that would have been impossible to attain during this time period for a single woman. Indeed, Vivie has attended school with this shameful money.

This play is fascinating to examine because of the time period in which it was written: 1893. Late Victorian England. A repressed society with abject poverty and high moral standards. Yet lurking beneath the surface was a lascivious subculture. For context: The Jack the Ripper murders in London were just five years prior, and prostitutes in England had already long acquired a deviant reputation.

In the following scene from Act Two, we see a disagreement between Mrs. Warren and Vivie about Vivie's future with a potential marriage prospect: in this case, Frank, who has just left.

MRS. WARREN: Did you ever in your life hear anyone rattle on so? Isn't he a tease? Now that I think of it, dearie, don't you go encouraging him. I'm sure he's a regular good-for-nothing.
VIVIE: I'm afraid so. Poor Frank! I shall have to get rid of him; but I shall feel sorry for
him, though he's not worth it. That man Crofts does not seem to me to be good for much either: is he?
(She throws the books on the table rather roughly).
MRS. WARREN: What do you know of men, child, to talk that way about them? You'll have to make up your mind to see a good deal of Sir George Crofts, as he's a friend of mine.
VIVIE: Why? Do you expect that we shall be much together? You and I, I mean?
MRS. WARREN: Of course: until you're married. You're not going back to college again.
VIVIE: Do you think my way of life would suit you? I doubt it.
MRS. WARREN: Your way of life! What do you mean?
VIVIE: Has it really never occurred to you, mother, that I have a way of life like other people?

MRS. WARREN: What nonsense is this you're trying to talk? Do you want to shew your independence, now that you're a great little person at school? Don't be a fool, child.

VIVIE: That's all you have to say on the subject, is it, mother?

MRS. WARREN: Don't you keep on asking me questions like that. Hold your tongue. You and your way of life, indeed! What next? Your way of life will be what I please, so it will. I've been noticing these airs in you ever since you got that tripos or whatever you call it. If you think I'm going to put up with them you're mistaken; and the sooner you find out, the better. All I have to say on the subject, indeed! Do you know who you are speaking to, Miss?

VIVIE: No. Who are you? What are you?

MRS. WARREN: You young imp!

VIVIE: Everybody knows my reputation, my social standing, and the profession I intend to pursue. I know nothing about you. What is that way of life which you invite me to share with you and Sir George Crofts, pray?

MRS. WARREN: Take care. I shall do something I'll be sorry for after, and you too.

The scene carries on well after that. Shaw, the playwright, has put in a tense scene with some interesting revelations about character. The actors have plenty to work with in this scene, and the dialogue carries much in the way of action. Many actors add notes to their scripts determining which action verb fits the moment best for them, so much of the analysis we did above with our made-up attorney script can be applied by you, the writer. Adding in the action verbs as a form of margin note can be very helpful to determine whether or not a line is playable. Better yet, it can help you determine if you're maximizing conflict. This is important especially on the external level—we can see what the character is doing as a tactic, whether on screen or on stage.

Let's see what the action verbs might look like in context when applied as a note (*in italics and caps*).

MRS. WARREN: Did you ever in your life hear anyone rattle on so? Isn't he a tease? *(MOCK)* Now that I think of it, dearie, don't you go encouraging him. *(WARN)* I'm sure he's a regular good-for-nothing. *(BELITTLE)*

VIVIE: I'm afraid so. Poor Frank! I shall have to get rid of him; but I shall feel sorry for

him, though he's not worth it. That man Crofts does not seem to me to be good for much either: is he? *(REBUT)*

(She throws the books on the table rather roughly).

MRS. WARREN: What do you know of men, child, to talk that way about them? *(MOCK)* You'll have to make up your mind to see a good deal of Sir George Crofts, as he's a friend of mine. *(FOREWARN)*

VIVIE: Why? Do you expect that we shall be much together? You and I, I mean? *(ANALYZE)*

MRS. WARREN: Of course: until you're married. You're not going back to college again. *(WARN)*

VIVIE: Do you think my way of life would suit you? I doubt it. *(BELITTLE)*

MRS. WARREN: Your way of life! What do you mean? *(INQUIRE)*

VIVIE: Has it really never occurred to you, mother, that I have a way of life like other people? *(CLARIFY)*

MRS. WARREN: What nonsense is this you're trying to talk? Do you want to shew your independence, now that you're a great little person at school? Don't be a fool, child. *(MOCK)*

VIVIE: That's all you have to say on the subject, is it, mother? *(MOCK)*

MRS. WARREN: Don't you keep on asking me questions like that. Hold your tongue. You and your way of life, indeed!

What next? Your way of life will be what I please, so it will. I've been noticing these airs in you ever since you got that tripos or whatever you call it. If you think I'm going to put up with them you're mistaken; and the sooner you find out, the better. All I have to say on the subject, indeed! Do you know who you are speaking to, Miss? *(SUBJUGATE)*

VIVIE: No. Who are you? What are you? *(BLAME)*

MRS. WARREN: You young imp!

VIVIE: Everybody knows my reputation, my social standing, and the profession I intend to pursue. I know nothing about you. What is that way of life which you invite me to share with you and Sir George Crofts, pray? *(BLAME)*

MRS. WARREN: Take care. I shall do something I'll be sorry for after, and you too. *(WARN)*

Certainly, these verb choices differ for each actor and each director. That's the whole point of being an actor: making choices that are in line with the director's vision, and these choices are key to the actor's approach. It's often why they are cast in the role in the first place. But what this example does is demonstrate *how* to apply this exercise. I do this with everything I write—*after* I write the first draft. As I mentioned, this is a revision process exercise, and it's one on which I rely heavily to determine if the dialogue I have written maximizes its potential.

So, that's how it works in a script—both screenplay and stage play. But how does it work in prose? Can the exercise be applied to novel and short story writing? Absolutely! In fact, I consider this part of the revision process vital to my prose writing. I love to envision that these lines are being uttered in a film, and I examine the dramatic function of each utterance. As we look through a couple of examples from novels, I want to preface with the overarching question I ask myself about each line of dialogue in a prose work: **What compels this character to speak?** Why not stay quiet? Why not describe the scene instead? Why do we have to hear the character's voice? What does it say about the character to say these words in this manner at this time? This is where examining the tactics becomes handy and productive. You will implicitly answer this question for each line of dialogue *and* engage thoroughly with each character in your novel or short story.

We'll take a look at two examples of prose to explore how this technique works for novels and short stories. The first one we'll look at is Charlotte Brönte's *Jane Eyre*, which I referenced earlier. In the following excerpt, Mr. Rochester, after lying about an engagement to Blanche Ingram in order to arouse jealousy in Jane, confesses his love for Jane and his desire to marry her. First, the excerpt without any annotations so you get a good sense of the scene:

"Come to my side, Jane, and let us explain and understand one another."

"I will never again come to your side; I am torn away now, and cannot return."

"But, Jane, I summon you as my wife; it is you only I intend to marry."

I was silent; I thought he mocked me.

"Come, Jane—come hither."

"Your bride stands between us." He rose, and with a stride reached me.

"My bride is here," he said, again drawing me to him, "because my equal is here, and my likeness. Jane, will you marry me?"

Still I did not answer, and still I writhed myself from his grasp; for I was still incredulous.

"Do you doubt me, Jane?"

"Entirely."

"You have no faith in me?"

"Not a whit."

"Am I a liar in your eyes?" he asked, passionately. "Little sceptic, you *shall* be convinced. What love have I for Miss Ingram? None, and that you know. What love has she for me? None, as

I have taken pains to prove; I caused a rumor to reach her that my fortune was not a third of what was supposed, and after that I presented myself to see the result; it was coldness both from her and her mother. I would not—I could not—marry Miss Ingram. You—you strange—you almost unearthly thing! I love as my own flesh. You—poor and obscure, and small and plain, as you are I entreat to accept me as a husband."

"What, me!" I ejaculated, beginning in his earnestness—and especially in his incivility—to credit his sincerity; "me, who have not a friend in the world but you—if you are my friend; not a shilling but what you have given me?"

"You, Jane. I must have you for my own—entirely my own. Will you be mine? Say yes, quickly."

"Mr. Rochester, let me look at your face; turn to the moonlight."

"Why?"

"Because I want to read your countenance; turn!"

"There you will find it scarcely more legible than a crumpled, scratched page. Read on; only make haste, for I suffer."

Now that you have an understanding and feeling for the scene, I'll add in the action verb annotations:

"Come to my side, Jane, and let us explain and understand one another." *(COMMAND)*

"I will never again come to your side; I am torn away now, and cannot return." *(DENY)*

"But, Jane, I summon you as my wife; it is you only I intend to marry." *(PLEAD)*

I was silent; I thought he mocked me.

"Come, Jane—come hither." *(COMMAND)*

"Your bride stands between us." *(DOUBT)*

He rose, and with a stride reached me.

"My bride is here," he said, again drawing me to him, "because my equal is here, and my likeness. Jane, will you marry me?" *(PERSUADE)*

Still I did not answer, and still I writhed myself from his grasp; for I was still incredulous.

"Do you doubt me, Jane?" *(INQUIRE)*

"Entirely." *(DOUBT)*

"You have no faith in me?" *(ENTREAT)*

"Not a whit." *(DOUBT)*

"Am I a liar in your eyes?" *(ENTREAT)* he asked, passionately. "Little sceptic, you *shall* be convinced. What love have I for Miss Ingram? None, and that you know. What love has she for me? None, as I have taken pains to prove; I caused a rumor to reach her that my fortune was not a third of what was supposed, and after that I presented myself to see the result; it was coldness both from her and her mother. I would not—I could not—marry Miss Ingram. You—you strange—you almost unearthly thing! I love as my own flesh. You—poor and obscure, and small and plain, as you are *(CONVINCE)*—I entreat to accept me as a husband." *(ENTREAT)*

"What, me!" I ejaculated, beginning in his earnestness—and especially in his incivility—to credit his sincerity; "me, who have not a friend in the world but you—if you are my friend; not a shilling but what you have given me?" *(DOUBT)*

"You, Jane. I must have you for my own—entirely my own. Will you be mine? Say yes, quickly." *(BADGER)*

"Mr. Rochester, let me look at your face; turn to the moonlight." *(EXAMINE)*

"Why?" *(SUPPRESS)*

"Because I want to read your countenance; turn!" *(COMMAND)*

"There you will find it scarcely more legible than a crumpled, scratched page. Read on; only make haste, for I suffer." *(SURRENDER TO)*

You may have noticed in this excerpt the extent to which prose can really fill in the blanks with regard to tactic—how often we get to read the inner mindset of the characters to understand their tactics a bit more than we might see in a film, play or television program. That's the possibility of the medium, and we certainly see that at work here in this excerpt. Let's analyze some of the external tactics I've enumerated above and discuss some of the possibilities.

This scene is the height of what already has been a few pages of banter regarding the prospect of marriage. Jane still believes Rochester is to marry Miss Ingram, and rightfully so, for he's implied it heavily and Jane has implied her love for him. Through the entire exchange, Jane believes it would be best for her to leave his home of Thornfield, however much it grieves her. Jane very much asserts her power as a free woman of "independent mind" (as she says), so Rochester recognizes he has to tread lightly. Interestingly, many of these lines of dialogue are not followed by prose descriptions of their tone. They are powerful lines of dialogue that encapsulate the tone, allowing readers to lose themselves in the conversation. This comes with the territory when tactics are clear.

Rochester's first line *commands* Jane to understand with the line "Come to my side, Jane, and let us explain and understand one another." It might be tempting here to mark *invite* as the tactic at work, but *invite* seems to imply a bit more subjugation than I believe Rochester is at during this portion of the conversation. Jane's line "I will never again come to your side; I am torn away now, and cannot return" suggests her independent spirit brewing under the surface, but the external tactic here is immediate; she *denies* Rochester the opportunity to explain.

Rochester's next line has him cut to the chase with what he wants to say: "But, Jane, I summon you as my wife; it is you only I intend to marry." He *pleads* with her to understand why he wants to talk to her and explain—the latter portion of the line is the explanation. We know this line catches Jane off-guard with the prose description: *I was silent; I thought he mocked me.* This bit of internal monologue is key: it helps us understand Jane's behavior through the remaining part of the scene. Notice Brönte does not dwell here. The brevity of the description allows the scene to play out with the urgency and immediacy it needs.

Rochester's response to Jane's silence is "Come, Jane—come hither." Again, he commands Jane to come to him so he can explain. Certainly there's an undercurrent to why he doubles down on asking her to come nearer to him instead of acknowledging the silence; that's coming up in the next chapter as we explore the subtext. Jane's response casts *doubt* on his intentions still with the line "your bride stands between us." Again, she believes he mocks her. It's interesting that she maintains this action throughout much of the scene remaining. Her skepticism is dominant throughout, and this manifests in her continued *doubt* of everything Rochester says.

Rochester does get up and move toward her, taking Jane in his arms. His next line is "my bride is here"..."because my equal is here, and my likeness. Jane, will you marry me?" These lines could be viewed as an attempt to *persuade* her. Certainly there are other, softer tactics at play here, but his attempt to *persuade* her remains on the surface. Jane, however, is not having it as she frees herself from his hold. Rochester *inquires* about her doubt quite directly and then *entreats* her with his line "you have no faith in me." Jane's tactic to both of his actions here is again to *doubt*. *Entreat* seems a suitable tactic for Rochester because he seems to ask her earnestly.

Indeed, Rochester's next tactic remains *entreat* with the line "am I a liar in your eyes?" It then shifts to *convince* for the duration of his long speech to her as he feels the sting of her *doubt*. Then, he ends that speech with a direct *entreating* "to accept me as a husband." Jane's response is quite hasty, especially given the silent and laconic responses she's had: "What, me!" I ejaculated, beginning in his earnestness—and especially in his incivility—to credit his sincerity; "me, who have not a friend in the world but you—if you are my friend; not a shilling but what you have given me?" Here, we have more *doubt*, but it's a quick interjection before we have a bit of prose description. She continues to *doubt* him after.

Rochester doubles down; he's not taking no for an answer, despite her remaining disbelief of his intentions: "you, Jane. I must have you for my own—entirely my own. Will you be mine? Say yes, quickly." *Badger* seems a strong verb here, but at this point in the scene, Rochester is getting desperate. Jane must sense his desperation since she asks to *examine* Mr. Rochester's face. His response of *"why?"* is a way to *suppress* her doubt; perhaps even *dissuade* would work here as a surface tactic. Jane *commands* him to let her examine him with the line "because I want to read your countenance; turn!" Rochester certainly feels resigned to whatever Jane feels at this point; he feels he's tried what he can to make amends as he *surrenders to* her with the line "there you will find it scarcely more legible than a crumpled, scratched page. Read on; only make haste, for I suffer." You'll notice that *surrenders to* is actually two verbs, and that's okay. It is a **verb phrase** that still requires a direct object; Rochester *surrenders to* Jane. The action is done *to* Jane.

Jane Eyre has so many passages that could be explored in this same manner, but let's move on to something a little more contemporary. Let's look at an excerpt from Jameson Tabard's darkly comedic novel *The Scottish Bitch*—the modern update of *Macbeth* with drag queens. Many of the characters in the book are analogues for characters in the original play, so in this scene, Duffy (an analogue for Lady MacDuff) and Twatla (an analogue for MacDuff) are upset over the death of Cunny Corleone, an analogue for Banquo. In the scene, Cunny Corleone's body has been discovered at the Holy Land Experience, and it has been suspected Latrine Dion (an analogue for Macbeth) has killed her to make it easier for her to win the title in a drag queen competition. Here is the excerpt, with the prose included.

Twatla made it to the Holy Land Experience in under twenty minutes. Duffy speedwalked to intercept her and locked her in a tight embrace.

"You shouldn't be here."

Twatla broke free. "That bitch."

"I know what you're thinking," said Duffy, as if a warning were the next words out of her mouth. "There's no proof yet that Latrine's the one behind this."

"Just two dead queens who were better than she'll ever be. Isn't that enough?" Twatla noticed there was no crime scene tape. No sign of a body. It must've been taken away.

Duffy put a hand on her shoulder. "It's just speculation. We don't know enough about Latrine's relationship with either of them, especially Cunny. Look. For all we know it was a hate crime."

Twatla crossed her arms. "A hate *losing* crime."

"It could've been Peyton."

"That fucking little murderous leprechaun."

"We can say they're persons of interest. We will investigate them for sure. But that's all we can do right now. They're just not charged with anything." Duffy turned Twatla's face toward hers. "You need to be clear on that."

The goal now, with this excerpt is, is for the writer to then isolate the sections with the dialogue and treat them as if they're lines in a script. This is what I call a **dialogue pass.** Performing a dialogue pass ensures you have dialogue that maximizes conflict for your characters. It allows us to spot the tactics each character uses to achieve both their immediate objective and their long-term superobjective. So, let's perform the same exercise we did above in our scripts with the dialogue in this prose scene:

Twatla made it to the Holy Land Experience in under twenty minutes. Duffy speedwalked to intercept her and locked her in a tight embrace.

"You shouldn't be here." *(WARN)*

Twatla broke free. "That bitch." *(ACCUSE)*

"I know what you're thinking," *(WARN)* said Duffy, as if a warning were the next words out of her mouth. "There's no proof yet that Latrine's the one behind this." *(WARN)*

"Just two dead queens who were better than she'll ever be. Isn't that enough?" *(ACCUSE)* Twatla noticed there was no crime scene tape. No sign of a body. It must've been taken away.

Duffy put a hand on her shoulder. "It's just speculation. We don't know enough about Latrine's relationship with either of them, especially Cunny. Look. For all we know it was a hate crime." *(MOLLIFY)*

Twatla crossed her arms. "A hate *losing* crime." *(ACCUSE)*

"It could've been Peyton." *(DEFLECT)*

"That fucking little murderous leprechaun." *(ACCUSE)*

"We can say they're persons of interest. We will investigate them for sure. But that's all we can do right now. They're just not charged with anything." *(MOLLIFY)* Duffy turned Twatla's face toward hers. "You need to be clear on that." *(WARN)*

This scene is a good example because the tactics stay pretty consistent. We can see what each character's goals are with the words in parenthesis. Twatla's goals and tactics are really to blow off steam. She's certain she knows who the killer is. Duffy is fairly certain as well, but since her job is to investigate the crime, she has an ethical obligation to keep the investigation open. Additionally, she has to ensure Twatla won't openly accuse those she suspects; that could derail the investigation. It's important to note that we understand the anger Twatla feels, but I haven't used any adjectives in the parenthesis. An adjective like "angry" here isn't strong enough to address the tactic. Anger is not a verb; therefore, it's a poor way to analyze the tactic. Moreover, what this does is specify the action to define the conflict more clearly. Opposing tactics or differing tactics between your characters allows you to see the shape and direction of the scene, its energy, and its importance to the overall story. When a line doesn't have enough of a clear tactic, I either change it or eliminate it.

EXERCISE #4

When you have finished a draft of your script or novel, the first thing you should do is take a break. Come back to it fresh after you've given yourself some time away from it, and reread the whole work from start to finish. Then, go back to the beginning and isolate each line of dialogue. Pencil in or identify the tactic in each line of dialogue. Don't worry about getting it perfect—just identify what you think each character's external objective for each line of dialogue. You will absolutely have the same verb in certain sections. You can absolutely have different verbs in others. If you find yourself haggling over a specific action verb application, that may mean you have a poor or unclear line of dialogue. It may mean your line has a vague sense of conflict. Perhaps put a question mark if you're unsure of which verb to apply, but don't scratch out the line all together just yet. It *may* get altered or deleted in the next draft you write, but we need to perform another test on it before we do anything.

You may find this process to be painstaking, but the level of detail here is key, and once you complete it, your work is pretty darn solid. You are scrutinizing every uttered word on the page, everything your characters say. That improves characterization and improves your story. You'll get to map the plot better, and you'll weigh each word in the line to ensure you're getting the most out of your dialogue.

To perform this exercise properly, I like to physically print out my manuscript. Then, I like to use colored pens or pencils to write the verbs beside the lines. That allows me to see clearly exactly what I've written and what the actions are. I also get a better sense of the pacing and the effect the dialogue is having. However, you don't have to print out the manuscript if you don't want to—you certainly can use italics, bold print, or colored fonts. Whatever works best for you. I would suggest that whatever color you choose to represent a character's external objective, you stick with that color. In the next chapter, we'll be discussing the character's *internal* objective, and that might require a different color.

CHAPTER 3

THE CHARACTER'S INTERNAL SUPEROBJECTIVE

While the previous chapter was about the character's *external* superobjective, this chapter is about the character's *internal* superobjective. This superobjective concerns the character's *need*—what they *must* accomplish in order to achieve the external superobjective. Therefore, these two objectives are closely related. Whereas the external superobjective was something tangible, however, the internal is usually something more abstract. The internal can range from things like overcoming a vice, like alcoholism, to learning to depend on oneself. Because this *need* tends to be more universal in nature, meaning many readers or viewers can identify with this trait, the internal superobjective usually carries the **theme**.

The internal superobjective involves a deeper sense of who your character is. They have a deeper, more personal obstacle they must overcome—perhaps that aforementioned *hamartia*, or tragic flaw. It can make your character more likeable (or unlikeable). Most importantly, it gives the audience or reader a *reason* to root for this character to achieve his or her external superobjective, or *want*. Because we identify with this character's struggle, we *want* to see them successful. We want that moment of satisfaction, or perhaps **catharsis** when they overcome that deep-seated obstacle. Let's revisit some examples from the previous chapter and examine how much depth and meaning is added to these stories by analyzing the internal needs of the protagonists.

In *The Wonderful Wizard of Oz* by L. Frank Baum and its subsequent film, we examined Dorothy's external superobjective: She wants to get home to Kansas. It could further be expressed in the central dramatic question: *Will Dorothy return home?* Indeed, that's what her whole stated journey is. But what does she have to do to get home? She has to figure something out, and Glinda tells us that she's always had it—the ruby slippers. These ruby slippers are a symbol that reminds Dorothy that *she's always carried home with her*, for it manifests in her newfound friends. That's the theme: you always carry home with you wherever you go. The values. The experiences. The love. In fact, each of her new companions learns they've always had the very thing they longed for: a brain, a heart, and courage.

In *Lord of the Rings*, we expressed the central dramatic question as *Will Frodo save the Shire (by destroying the ring)?* Frodo's whole stated journey is to accomplish this herculean task. But what is it that Frodo must do to accomplish this goal? He must *summon the courage to make the choice* to destroy the ring. Naturally, this goes deeper. He has the support of his friends, and the circumstances of his being a hobbit make him less likely to be seduced by the power of the ring, but in the end, it's the courage to go on the quest that gets him there. Thus, the *need(s)* for Frodo is to find courage and make a choice. Having courage in the most dire circumstances is a major theme in the novels and the films, and not surprisingly, we see Frodo overcoming many obstacles that test his courage. Moreover, the context in which Tolkien wrote the series—World War I and the nascent stages of what would become World War II—informs this theme.

In Jameson Tabard's darkly comedic novel *The Scottish Bitch*, protagonist Latrine Dion's central dramatic question can be expressed here as *Will Latrine win the Grand Dame Competition?* In order to do this, she must overcome her tragic flaw—her *hamartia*—and this carries her internal superobjective. Her tragic flaw is that she is vain and has delusions of grandeur. If she does not overcome this hubris, it will destroy her. Indeed, since this is based on *Macbeth*, we know Latrine will not overcome this tragic flaw. She will succumb to her fate. One of the major themes in this novel is *vanity can destroy ambition*.

In Disney's *Coco*, Miguel dreams of becoming a musician in a family where music is banned, due to a generations-long understanding that a distant ancestor, his great-great grandfather, abandoned his family for musical stardom. Miguel's central dramatic question can be expressed as *Will Miguel return home (to the Land of the Living)?* Returning home comes with the realization that he won't have music, so he must learn the truth about his family. While that's important—the root of this quest for the truth is that he must remain true to himself. He cannot give up that love of music. Therefore, a major theme in the film is *remaining true to oneself* and Miguel's internal superobjective is to find the truth of his family. They are very closely related.

If you find yourself disagreeing with some of these major themes in these works, that's perfectly valid. There are many more themes in these stories than what I've listed here. Some of them even have themes related to secondary characters and antagonists. Some of them have themes that are more circumstantial and are related more to how the reader sees the characters. But what I have outlined here are some brief examples of how these themes connect to an internal *need* of the protagonist in each of these stories—an obstacle they need to overcome to achieve that external goal. This will help inform the dialogue choices within individual scenes, as the characters find themselves face-to-face with the obstacles and vices that may prevent them from achieving their long-term goals. Since the previous chapter in this book discussed tactics as they relate to the character's external goals, this chapter will discuss actions as they relate to their internal ones. Their needs. Their convictions. Who they are as living, breathing entities. This will also be where you set up or foreshadow moments that will come later. This is where you'll discover your pacing issues. This is where the real fun of revising dialogue is.

SUBTEXT

Ask any English instructor, and they probably each have a different definition for this term. Reading between the lines. Hidden meanings. Unspoken truths. The basic gist of subtext is that it's often what is *really* meant by a line of dialogue. It is an underlying intention, meaning, idea, or theme. Subtext also reflects the three character profiles (psychological, physiological, and sociological) that were mentioned in Part One of this book. Subtext is important because it gives us depth to a character. The reader can "read between the lines." The audience can make assumptions about the characters—guesses about qualities or secrets that might not be readily apparent.

Actors especially love playing with subtext. In fact, good actors will often search the line for all its potential meanings while studying the script. A line layered with different ideas and intentions allows the actor to discover nuances about their character and allows them to dig deeper into the role. This becomes especially important for actors doing plays for extended periods of time. I've talked to so many actors (and experienced this myself), where a new discovery happens in the moment with a line because its delivery felt different or resonated in a different way to elicit a new reaction from the audience. It can allow the actor to discover depth that perhaps even the writer and director didn't realize was there.

The key word with subtext is **connotation.** What feelings does the line elicit? What does it imply? What intentions are present?

Let's examine subtext on a smaller scale. Take a line like "Shut up." On the surface, someone uttering this line might intend for the other person to stop talking immediately. It may carry connotations of hostility and anger, perhaps even a threatening tone. But this line could just as easily be said in a joking, playful manner. Maybe in a dismissive manner. It all depends on the circumstances and the intention.

Subtext does not have to be written. Body language can convey subtext. Gestures can convey subtext. Even blocking—the placement and movement of actors within a scene—can convey subtext. Camera angles, proximity, and movement conveys subtext. Cutting from a scene conveys subtext. Prose description and point of view in a novel conveys subtext.

Subtext is the result of exploring the inner life of a character. Shades of meaning come from a well-written line of dialogue in a novel. It can be delivered in myriad ways from a strong actor who understands his or her role in a play, film or television series. To convey as much subtext as possible in a line, it's important to understand how to craft it.

OBJECTIVES ON A SMALLER SCALE

Now that we've discussed the importance of subtext and the importance of the internal superobjective as it relates to the external, let's examine how this functions within the context of scene objectives. As a reminder, a **scene objective** is a short-term goal your character wants to achieve within the context of a scene or a sequence. In a novel, this objective may take place over the course of a chapter or a section, or even a few chapters. In any medium, the scene objective for your character should connect, to some extent, to your character's larger external superobjective. Sometimes, the scene objective belies an **internal objective,** a secret—an ulterior motive. Sometimes this internal objective conveys a subconscious goal, a want or need. It could be something not explicitly referenced in the text. It may not even be something the characters know about themselves. It could be something an actor or director discovers about the role later in their rehearsal process. It's important to note that **not every line will have an internal objective.** However, if one or more internal objectives are present, an actor will likely play with that subtext.

Let's return to our attorney story *Molly Carpenter, Esquire.* As mentioned in the previous chapter, Molly's external superobjective is to win her case. William, her assistant, has plans to see his friend for happy hour, a friend who has flown into town for the weekend and whom he hasn't seen in two years. Those are their stated external goals. Read over the scene again, and see if you can determine any other underlying tensions. That will serve as the basis of exploring the subtext.

Molly: Where are you going?

Will: It's 5:00, Ms. Carpenter. Wherever I want.

Molly: Any chance I can convince you to stay?

Will: Not really.

Molly: I need you to stay.

Will: From nine to five each day, with the exception of my lunch break, you get to tell me what to do. After that, you're on my time.

Molly: I know it seems like I've been really stressed out lately, and I know I've been taking it out on people, but…

Will: It's now 5:01. You can tell me about your stresses in the morning if you'd like. Until then, have a good night.

Molly: Wait.

Will stops.

Molly: I'm willing to pay you overtime.

Will: That you want to pay me overtime tells me you're not looking for just an hour more of work. So again, I'll see you tomorrow.

Molly: Double time. I'll pay you double time.

Will: You don't get it. I have plans, Molly. It's Friday. Contrary to how I might make it seem, I don't live to work here.

Molly: I'm sorry for treating you like garbage.

Will: Okay, that's a start. I'm kind of—.

Molly: Surprised. I know. It's a new leaf.

Will: You really need me to stay.

Molly: I do.

Will: Why all of a sudden do you trust my judgment and work ethic enough to want me to stay?

Molly: I always have. I know I have a funny way of showing it.

Will: Funny is what you're calling it.

Molly: Not funny, but… you know what I mean.

Will: Double time is still on the table.

Molly: It is.

Will: Okay, let me text my buddies I'll be two hours late. I'll owe them a full round of drinks now, and not at the happy hour price.

Molly: Two hours? What if I need you to stay longer?

Will: Two hours, Ms. Carpenter.

Molly: Right. And you can call me Molly even though you're on the clock.

Will: Two hours starts now.

If you're sensing Will is a bit rude, even insubordinate, you're right. He definitely doesn't care if he loses his job, and he doesn't care if Molly fires him for any reason. That tone is prevalent throughout the scene. However, as mentioned in the previous chapter, the tone does shift on his part. It also shifts on her part. If you noticed Molly was a bit desperate in this scene, you're definitely right. She stands to lose a lot if Will doesn't stay. But if you noticed there feels like an implied history here, you're absolutely right. And that's what's worth exploring.

Let's take a look at what this scene might look like when we apply the same exercise in the previous chapter—the verb exercise—again, only this time the verb indicates a subtextual goal, something the character might consciously or unconsciously be doing with the line.

Molly: Where are you going?

Will: It's 5:00, Ms. Carpenter. Wherever I want. *(REBEL)*

Molly: Any chance I can convince you to stay? *(SELF-DISCIPLINE)*

Will: Not really.

Molly: I need you to stay. *(PLEAD)*

Will: From nine to five each day, with the exception of my lunch break, you get to tell me what to do. After that, you're on my time. *(AVENGE)*

Molly: I know it seems like I've been really stressed out lately, and I know I've been taking it out on people, but... *(EMPATHIZE)*

Will: It's now 5:01. You can tell me about your stresses in the morning if you'd like. Until then, have a good night. *(DISMISS)*

Molly: Wait.

Will stops.

Molly: I'm willing to pay you overtime. *(PLEAD; SWEETEN)*

Will: That you want to pay me overtime tells me you're not looking for just an hour more of work. So again, I'll see you tomorrow. *(PERSIST; FORTIFY)*

Molly: Double time. I'll pay you double time.

Will: You don't get it. I have plans, Molly. It's Friday. Contrary to how I might make it seem, I don't live to work here. *(SUBVERT)*

Molly: I'm sorry for treating you like garbage. *(GROVEL)*

Will: Okay, that's a start. I'm kind of—.

Molly: Surprised. I know. It's a new leaf.

Will: You really need me to stay.

Molly: I do. *(CONFESS)*

Will: Why all of a sudden do you trust my judgment and work ethic enough to want me to stay? *(BLAME)*

Molly: I always have. I know I have a funny way of showing it.

Will: Funny is what you're calling it.

Molly: Not funny, but... you know what I mean. *(GROVEL)*

Will: Double time is still on the table. *(PERSIST)*

Molly: It is.

Will: Okay, let me text my buddies I'll be two hours late. I'll owe them a full round of drinks now, and not at the happy hour price. *(BLAME)*

Molly: Two hours? What if I need you to stay longer? *(PROD)*

Will: Two hours, Ms. Carpenter.

Molly: Right. And you can call me Molly even though you're on the clock. *(EQUALIZE)*

Will: Two hours starts now. *(CONTROL)*

The goal with this exercise versus the one in the previous chapter is that these verbs should be different from those you've already used. Not only should they be different, but strive to make them as opposite as you can. Also, you'll notice that there may be many verbs you could use to convey the character's internal goal. That's a good thing. That means you've got a line that could be interpreted a number of different ways, and that sense of ambiguity makes reading it more fulfilling. The ambiguity allows the actor a greater sense of creative freedom in making choices for the character and the line. It also makes for a more fulfilling audience experience. The audience is more engaged in the story because of the ambiguity.

If you printed out your script or novel for the verb exercise in the last chapter, maybe you've handwritten the external verbs beside the line in pen or pencil. Consider using another color to write in the internal, more subtextual verbs beside it. This technique will allow you to see better whether or not a line is working.

You can certainly enumerate several verbs in parenthesis for each line or action beat. However, simply listing one or two already lets you know you've got a line that works well. That's the point of this whole exercise: Testing the line to maximize its function. Now, if you come across a line where there doesn't seem to be a subtextual intention, make an annotation of some kind. Circle or highlight it. There may be a problem with that line, or there may not. We'll explore lines like this in a later chapter.

Let's analyze some of the verb choices in the aforementioned scene. After Molly asks her first question (the first line of the scene), we see Will's reaction as a declaration. His external goal here is to avoid Molly, which already carries with it some specific connotations. However, an opposite choice of a verb that could work to give this line more depth would be *rebel*. The simple act of rebelling here—his declaration that he's leaving regardless of what she says—implies much more of a backstory. We perhaps have had several instances where Molly has been rude, demanding, impatient—you name it. Will is likely tired of his mistreatment and doesn't care what she thinks. If we play with the unspoken objective here that Will is looking for another job, this makes his rebellion feel more safe. It's a powerful thing for Will to know he has options and doesn't need to take the abuse for much longer. Molly's reaction to this is to self-discipline. She wants to react in a much stronger way, especially if the actor delivers the line in an obviously rude or insubordinate tone. But Molly **needs** him to stay and help. If she gets angry or upset in any way, she risks losing his assistance at a moment she really needs it. Moreover, she understands she's been difficult. She has had that rock bottom moment—an anagnorisis, or recognition—that helps her realize what she's done wrong all this time and what she needs to do to correct it. She also doesn't want to come across as desperate. She's still his boss and has a sense of pride after all. Therefore, these lines carry various connotations. They have subtext. They're effective lines of dialogue. In this case, this exercise demonstrates these lines have a depth of characterization, an important element of compelling dialogue.

The tactics change, just as they did with the external objectives. Molly's next internal action is to plead. She probably doesn't do so in a groveling way, but it's what she really means. Still trying to maintain her dignity, she tells him *I need you to stay*. It's a declarative statement of what she really needs that still keeps her authority but also lets Will know she's in dire straits. For Will's response, I've chosen *avenge*. At first glance, this verb seems an odd choice. He's not really avenging anyone but himself here, and the external goal is really to *lecture* Molly. Basically, he's reminding her of the tacit agreement of his work schedule and his responsibilities when he's on the clock. He's right. Since he's not on the clock, he's not beholden to her wishes. But with the choice of *avenge* as an internal, subtextual verb, we have the implication of backstory. This verb suggests that somewhere in the recent past, Molly has caught Will not doing work at his desk. Perhaps he was paying his bills or on social media. He probably incurred some kind of lecture from Molly about his abusing her potential for making money on her billable time. Now, Will has the opportunity to turn the tables. He can get a form of revenge on Molly since he probably is starting to recognize she's desperate, and again, he doesn't care if he loses his job.

The implied backstory here is key. Writing good dialogue for a script means maximizing the potential of each line. Here, we get a sense of what has happened in the past between these two characters without having to explain their relationship. Lines that explain details or backstory often feel forced. We call these lines **expositional**. They try to provide exposition by spoonfeeding character details, and it makes for boring scenes that lack momentum. But if you focus these lines of dialogue on subtextual motivations, you maintain the conflict needed to propel the scene forward.

Case in point: Will could have very easily responded to Molly with a line like, *You told me I only had to work between nine and five and those were my hours* instead of *From nine to five each day, with the exception of my lunch break, you get to tell me what to do. After that, you're on my time.* That's spoonfeeding detail; moreover, it makes Will seem a bit weak. Keeping Molly in a powerful position and Will in a weaker position makes this scene dull. She's already in a powerful position by virtue of being his boss. It's much more interesting for her to be in a weaker position in the scene. Thus, including the subtextual action of *avenge* empowers and compels Will to respond in the way he does.

Molly perhaps senses Will's rebellion and his throwing her own bossiness back at her. This motivates the next line: *I know it seems like I've been really stressed out lately, and I know I've been taking it out on people, but…* This line carries with it a type of confession. She knows she needs to mollify (no pun intended) Will by *empathizing* with him. That means she needs to come clean with her treatment of him, but to do so in a way that still helps her achieve her external goal of convincing him to stay. So, here, directly apologizing feels inappropriate because that doesn't feel earned. Empathizing with him at this point in the scene works better because the circumstances don't require that strong a tactic yet.

What makes this scene get even more interesting is the increase in conflict. Will doesn't take to Molly's strategy of empathizing, and instead, he doubles down on his next line: *It's now 5:01. You can tell me about your stresses in the morning if you'd like. Until then, have a good night.* This line tells us Will knows he really has nothing to lose at this point by dismissing her as such. On the surface, he's still evading her, but under the surface, he's usurped the power in the scene and made Molly realize her tactic isn't strong enough yet. The only moment of blocking in the scene is what I included here: *Will stops.* That tells the director and the actors Will is heading for the door or doing something similar at this point—something that forces Molly to change her tactic immediately.

Notice that on her next line, *I'm willing to pay you overtime*, I show two subtextual verbs. On the one hand, the severity of the verb has increased from before. Now, Molly is *pleading*. However, she's also asserting a little more power here by *sweetening* the deal. If you feel *negotiate* is an appropriate verb here, you're absolutely correct. That's another aspect of what's going on here. Moreover, Molly, to some extent, is attempting to reclaim a little bit of power in the scene as well, perhaps subconsciously. So the choice to play this section of the scene as *usurping* would also be an interesting approach for an actor. The sheer number of verbs that work for this line tells us we have a strong, playable line of dialogue. It also reveals how much depth we have to Molly's characterization.

Will's response line is *That you want to pay me overtime tells me you're not looking for just an hour more of work. So again, I'll see you tomorrow.* For this line, again I've ascribed two subtextual verbs: *persist* and *fortify.* They're related verbs, yes, but Will is maintaining his strength in the scene, and he's also attempting to increase it. We know this because Molly's response of paying him *double time* comes from even more of a place of desperation. Will's response to this is *you don't get it,* and he proceeds to explain and clarify why he needs to go. Explain—even clarify—are surface verbs here, but *subvert* is where the underlying tension is. He still maintains his power with that line.

Notice that for Molly's apology line *I'm sorry for treating you like garbage,* I've included a really degrading verb for her: *grovel.* I have done this intentionally, for at this moment in the scene, she's completely lost and desperate. It's a rock bottom moment for her within the scene. It's also a moment where Will might feel some sympathy for her. Her next tactic, subtextually, is to *confess* to him that she really needs him. Will's response question is *why all of a sudden do you trust my judgment and work ethic enough to want me to stay?* I've chosen a specific verb here for Will for a reason. On the surface, he's questioning Molly's tactic. Under the surface, he certainly demonstrates a lack of faith in her. But that's not an active response. That feeling under the surface leans more to the adjectival feeling than to the action-oriented approach. If that line is weaponized and Will *blames* Molly for having had a lack of faith in him to that point, he still maintains the upper hand. Certainly, the line doesn't have to feel heavy-handed with the blame, but that's what's actually going on there. That's the subtext.

Will's *blame* continues through his next line: *Funny is what you're calling it.* Molly definitely feels like she's been in the wrong and still maintains her feeling that she's losing in the scene and will lose if Will does not stay. She continues to *grovel.* Will's response shows he's *persisting* when he says *double time is still on the table.* He's won the argument and keeps the upper hand. If you noticed that he sounds a little snide when he reverts back to *blaming* her, you're right. It is intended to be snide. The line *Okay, let me text my buddies I'll be two hours late. I'll owe them a full round of drinks now, and not at the happy hour price* is passive-aggressive; however, passive-aggressive is not a verb. To keep this action-oriented, having Will *blame* Molly for his having to pay more for drinks with his buddies is in line with his tactic during the last half of the scene. If you thought this line implies that he's *guilting* Molly, that's absolutely another playable action that works here. Again, we have a line that could be interpreted a number of ways and one that shows depth of character.

Molly's response is *Two hours? What if I need you to stay longer?* This line implies that she assumed Will would be staying later. It also reveals, to an extent, that she almost wants to revert back to the status quo in how she treats Will. But still, she knows she could lose his help at any time, so she's feeling out the answer to this question. She's *prodding*. Will maintains his firmness at the end of the scene and ends by asserting his *control*, even after Molly has *equalized* them by allowing him to call her by her first name.

Let's move on to another of our scenes from the last chapter, this one from *Mrs. Warren's Profession*. If you remember, this scene is a disagreement between Mrs. Warren and Vivie about Vivie's future with a potential marriage prospect: in this case, Frank, who has just left.

MRS. WARREN: Did you ever in your life hear anyone rattle on so? Isn't he a tease? Now that I think of it, dearie, don't you go encouraging him. I'm sure he's a regular good-for-nothing.
VIVIE: I'm afraid so. Poor Frank! I shall have to get rid of him; but I shall feel sorry for
him, though he's not worth it. That man Crofts does not seem to me to be good for much either: is he?
(She throws the books on the table rather roughly).
MRS. WARREN: What do you know of men, child, to talk that way about them? You'll have to make up your mind to see a good deal of Sir George Crofts, as he's a friend of mine.

VIVIE: Why? Do you expect that we shall be much together? You and I, I mean?

MRS. WARREN: Of course: until you're married. You're not going back to college again.

VIVIE: Do you think my way of life would suit you? I doubt it.

MRS. WARREN: Your way of life! What do you mean?

VIVIE: Has it really never occurred to you, mother, that I have a way of life like other people?

MRS. WARREN: What nonsense is this you're trying to talk? Do you want to shew your independence, now that you're a great little person at school? Don't be a fool, child.

VIVIE: That's all you have to say on the subject, is it, mother?

MRS. WARREN: Don't you keep on asking me questions like that. Hold your tongue. You and your way of life, indeed! What next? Your way of life will be what I please, so it will. I've been noticing these airs in you ever since you got that tripos or whatever you call it. If you think I'm going to put up with them you're mistaken; and the sooner you find out, the better. All I have to say on the subject, indeed! Do you know who you are speaking to, Miss?

VIVIE: No. Who are you? What are you?

MRS. WARREN: You young imp!

VIVIE: Everybody knows my reputation, my social standing, and the profession I intend to pursue. I know nothing about you. What is that way of life which you invite me to share with you and Sir George Crofts, pray?

MRS. WARREN: Take care. I shall do something I'll be sorry for after, and you too.

At this point in the play, Vivie does not know the true story of her parentage. She does not know who her father is, nor does she know the nature of her mother's. With this knowledge still outstanding for the audience of this play, this scene becomes quite pivotal. The tension mounts, and we almost get an admission from Mrs. Warren's about her salacious past. Let's take a look at what this scene might look like with the internal verbs applies here.

MRS. WARREN: Did you ever in your life hear anyone rattle on so? Isn't he a tease? *(MOCK; CONDEMN)* Now that I think of it, dearie, don't you go encouraging him. *(WARN; CONDESCEND)* I'm sure he's a regular good-for-nothing. *(BELITTLE; DISSUADE)*

VIVIE: I'm afraid so. Poor Frank! I shall have to get rid of him; but I shall feel sorry for
him, though he's not worth it. That man Crofts does not seem to me to be good for much either: is he? *(REBUT; BLAME)* (She throws the books on the table rather roughly.)

MRS. WARREN: What do you know of men, child, to talk that way about them? *(MOCK; REPRIMAND)* You'll have to make up your mind to see a good deal of Sir George Crofts, as he's a friend of mine. *(FOREWARN; HINT)*

VIVIE: Why? Do you expect that we shall be much together? You and I, I mean? *(ANALYZE; SUBVERT)*

MRS. WARREN: Of course: until you're married. You're not going back to college again. *(WARN; CONTROL)*

VIVIE: Do you think my way of life would suit you? I doubt it. *(BELITTLE; SELF-AGGRANDIZE)*

MRS. WARREN: Your way of life! What do you mean? *(INQUIRE; SEIZE)*

VIVIE: Has it really never occurred to you, mother, that I have a way of life like other people? *(CLARIFY; DECLARE)*

MRS. WARREN: What nonsense is this you're trying to talk? Do you want to shew your independence, now that you're a great little person at school? Don't be a fool, child. *(MOCK; CONDESCEND [implies power])*

VIVIE: That's all you have to say on the subject, is it, mother? *(MOCK; GOAD)*

MRS. WARREN: Don't you keep on asking me questions like that. Hold your tongue. You and your way of life, indeed! What next? Your way of life will be what I please, so it will. I've been noticing these airs in you ever since you got that tripos or whatever you call it. If you think I'm going to put up with them you're mistaken; and the sooner you find out, the better. All I have to say on the subject, indeed! Do you know who you are speaking to, Miss? *(SUBJUGATE; SEIZE)*

VIVIE: No. Who are you? What are you? *(BLAME; INQUIRE)*

MRS. WARREN: You young imp!

VIVIE: Everybody knows my reputation, my social standing, and the profession I intend to pursue. I know nothing about you. What is that way of life which you invite me to share with you and Sir George Crofts, pray? *(BLAME; GOAD)*

MRS. WARREN: Take care. I shall do something I'll be sorry for after, and you too. *(WARN; EVADE)*

Mrs. Warren's first line initially has *mock* as the external verb, which works well for what's going on surface-wise here. Mrs. Warren is mocking Frank here, but she's also condemning him as an ill-suited fit for Vivie. Mrs. Warren's next sentence can also be played a number of ways, but for the purposes of demonstration, I've chosen *condescend*, because at this point in her relationship with Vivie, Mrs. Warren is unaware of Vivie's feelings and demeanor. The next sentence includes *belittle* as the external verb from the previous chapter, but I've chosen *dissuade* as appropriate here. On the surface, Mrs. Warren aims to belittle Frank, but in essence, she's also discouraging Vivie from pursuing any relationship or entanglement with him. This particular line for Mrs. Warren is interesting because within the line, the tactic changes three times. Naturally, the actor does not have to play the line with all of those changing actions, but as a writer, it's important to understand the possibility, as well as putting in this test to determine if the line is maximizing its playable potential.

Vivie's next line is a rebuttal, and that was the verb I used in the previous chapter to define what is occurring on the surface. I've chosen *blame* as the subtextual verb here because the line implies Vivie does not want her mother fixing her up with men. This subtext is also implied by the suggest blocking indicated in the script: *She throws the books on the table rather roughly.* For actors, writers, and directors, when staging a scene, remember that blocking also carries with it multiple connotations. Now, the trend for playwrights is *not* to provide excessive blocking on the page unless it conveys some key information, and this type of blocking would probably not be considered crucial for a contemporary audience. But Shaw wrote in a much different time period, and this play was probably staged in exactly this manner. This type of blocking line would probably be considered more *suggested* than anything, though the nature of the action tells us a great deal about Vivie's internal thoughts here.

Mrs. Warren's response to Vivie's action here is with the line: What do you know of men, child, to talk that way about them? On the surface, she's mocking her daughter, but the line also feels like a reprimand. How dare Vivie question her mother's feelings toward a potential suitor? Mrs. Warren's tactic changes with the next line: You'll have to make up your mind to see a good deal of Sir George Crofts, as he's a friend of mine. This line externally conveys a forewarning, but it also has a good deal of foreshadowing in it; the truth of Mrs. Warren's relationship with Crofts will soon come out. "Friend" can be taken a number of ways.

Vivie response by questioning her mother: Why? Do you expect that we shall be much together? You and I, I mean? It's a bold statement. On the surface, she's analyzing the situation, even with the direct question (the verb *interrogate* is also appropriate here). But she's also subverting her mother's meddling. Mrs. Warren seems to understand the attempt at subversion, for she rebuts with the line: Of course: until you're married. You're not going back to college again. Externally, Mrs. Warren warns Vivie, almost as if she wants to tell Vivie to hold her tongue. But under this line lies a bit of control; Mrs. Warren is well aware Vivie has profited off of Mrs. Warren's profession. That, combined with her role as Vivie's mother gives her the feeling she has a right to *control* Vivie.

The conversation takes a turn here. Vivie asserts the line: do you think my way of life would suit you? I doubt it, in which she *belittles* her mother, *condescending* to her with the sharp remark. Both verbs would work here. In doing so, Vivie also self-aggrandizes. She feels an air of superiority about herself over Mrs. Warren. She's an independent woman, and her education has taught her that. Mrs. Warren can barely stand this response. With a line like: your way of life! What do you mean?, she *inquires*, perhaps aghast, at the supposition. What she's really doing here is seizing control of the situation. Vivie's line is a put-down, and Mrs. Warren is desperate to *seize* control of the conversation.

Let's take a look at Vivie's next line: Has it really never occurred to you, mother, that I have a way of life like other people? On the surface here, Vivie *clarifies* her meaning for Mrs. Warren. It's also possible to consider this line as part of the previous action beat, and if you thought that upon reading this scene, you're not wrong. Vivie still could also be *belittling* her mother with this line. Under the surface, though this line is actually a question, Vivie is making a *declaration* of her independence.

Mrs. Warren still attempts to maintain control of the scene with her next line, and it's possible to consider it a continuation of the same action beat as her previous line. But it occurs to me that Mrs. Warren is well aware of Vivie's attempts to assert her own independence. The line itself states it: What nonsense is this you're trying to talk? Do you want to shew your independence, now that you're a great little person at school? Don't be a fool, child. Mrs. Warren sees Vivie's condescension and throws it right back at her, mocking her and reminding her of her place—that she's a child. The condescending tone here implies

Mrs. Warren's perceived power and her unending attempt to maintain control in the scene.

This aggravates Vivie. She sees the mocking and uses the same tactic with the line: That's all you have to say on the subject, is it, mother? But if, while reading this scene the first time, this line felt like a trap, you'd be right. That's the underlying action here. Vivie *goads* her mother to get to the important part of the scene—the impending question Vivie has wanted for a long time. She lays the groundwork here for the direct question.

Mrs. Warren's response to Vivie here is: Don't you keep on asking me questions like that. Hold your tongue. You and your way of life, indeed! What next? Your way of life will be what I please, so it will. I've been noticing these airs in you ever since you got that tripos or whatever you call it. If you think I'm going to put up with them you're mistaken; and the sooner you find out, the better. All I have to say on the subject, indeed! Do you know who you are speaking to, Miss? The sentence *your way of life will be what I please* indicates Mrs. Warren intends to *subjugate* Vivie on the surface—to put her in her place. For one, Mrs. Warren does not like to be called out and for two, she still feels she has a degree of authority over Vivie for being her mother and for providing Vivie with the money and lifestyle she needed to get through school. Under the surface, Mrs. Warren still clings to the power, so *seize* feels appropriate for an internal verb. If you switched these two verbs—*subjugate* and *seize*—I wouldn't say you were wrong. For me, this late in the scene, it feels like Mrs. Warren is openly subjugating Vivie while clinging desperately to the power she once had; therefore, *seize* feels more subtextual.

The scene reaches its climax with Vivie's line: No. Who are you? What are you? Vivie does not know her true parentage yet, nor does she know the nature of her mother's profession. This line implies she suspects some impropriety. The tone of the line suggests she's legitimately inquiring about her mother's past, so *inquire* works as a subtextual verb here. What's on the surface is the outright *blame* as a response to her mother's attempt to subjugate her with the previous line. We know Mrs. Warren is indignant over this question, perhaps even cornered. Her response is: you young imp! For me, the verbs still remain the same actions as before with this line; however, if you suggested *insult* or something similar would work here, that's absolutely true. Mrs. Warren, however, still attempts to subjugate Vivie even in the face of such a prying question.

Vivie's next line is fascinating because she continues with the same external action—to blame her mother—but the subtext seems to change. The line is: Everybody knows my reputation, my social standing, and the profession I intend to pursue. I know nothing about you. What is that way of life which you invite me to share with you and Sir George Crofts, pray? She knows she has her mother riled up, so she strikes with a prying question. Therefore, *pry* certainly works here as a verb, but it doesn't feel quite proactive enough. *Goad* feels much more baiting.

It almost feels like there should be a beat after Vivie's line, like the weight of such a deep question sinks into Mrs. Warren. Her response tells us she's been cornered. She *warns* Vivie with the line: Take care. I shall do something I'll be sorry for after, and you too. That warning is pretty explicitly clear. However, what lurks beneath the surface is the evasion. Mrs. Warren does not want to answer that question, at least not yet. It will strip her of her power, perhaps causing shame for Vivie, and shame even for herself.

George Bernard Shaw's play *Mrs. Warren's Profession* is really a classic of the Victorian Era, a time when so much was hidden from society yet present just under the surface. Indeed, Victorian literature provides so many opportunities to test out this exercise—to determine what characters' hidden intentions are because so often characters are not going to say what they want or need to say. But they will imply it.

Now that we've examined how this internal verb exercise works with scripts, let's revisit the two novel excerpts from the last chapter to determine how we can apply the same exercise to test the prose. In our first excerpt, from Charlotte Brönte's *Jane Eyre*, Mr. Rochester, after attempting to arouse jealousy in Jane by lying about an engagement to Blanche Ingram, confesses his love for the titular heroine. As with before, I'll give you the opportunity to refresh your memory with the scene sans annotations:

"Come to my side, Jane, and let us explain and understand one another."

"I will never again come to your side; I am torn away now, and cannot return."

"But, Jane, I summon you as my wife; it is you only I intend to marry."

I was silent; I thought he mocked me.

"Come, Jane—come hither."

"Your bride stands between us."

He rose, and with a stride reached me.

"My bride is here," he said, again drawing me to him, "because my equal is here, and my likeness. Jane, will you marry me?"

Still I did not answer, and still I writhed myself from his grasp; for I was still incredulous.

"Do you doubt me, Jane?"

"Entirely."

"You have no faith in me?"

"Not a whit."

"Am I a liar in your eyes?" he asked, passionately. "Little sceptic, you *shall* be convinced. What love have I for Miss Ingram? None, and that you know. What love has she for me? None, as I have taken pains to prove; I caused a rumor to reach her that my fortune was not a third of what was supposed, and after that I presented myself to see the result; it was coldness both from her and her mother. I would not—I could not—marry Miss Ingram. You—you strange—you almost unearthly thing!

I love as my own flesh. You—poor and obscure, and small and plain, as you are—I entreat to accept me as a husband."

"What, me!" I ejaculated, beginning in his earnestness—and especially in his incivility—to credit his sincerity; "me, who have not a friend in the world but you—if you are my friend; not a shilling but what you have given me?"

"You, Jane. I must have you for my own—entirely my own. Will you be mine? Say yes, quickly."

"Mr. Rochester, let me look at your face; turn to the moonlight."

"Why?"

"Because I want to read your countenance; turn!"

"There you will find it scarcely more legible than a crumpled, scratched page. Read on; only make haste, for I suffer."

As we've seen with analyzing previous two excerpts of plays, connotation matters, and actors' choices very much play into how a line will be interpreted. With prose writing, we lack the actors' talent to bring the line to life, or even a director to guide our interpretation of the line. However, that doesn't mean we can't approach writing dialogue in prose in the same manner. Put yourself in the actors' shoes and make a bold choice for what you see as the possibilities for subtext in this passage. One of the great benefits to using this exercise with prose writing is the nature of the medium: We can get inside the character's heads, so the medium does not *rely* on dialogue; dialogue is a tool that helps us convey the story better. I've written entire prose fiction pieces without dialogue, and I've certainly read whole memoirs without any. Because of this, we can really see the importance of the question **what compels the character to speak?** Characters in novels speak because they *must* speak. Part of this exercises, particularly with determining subtextual verbs, is understanding *why* they speak.

As with the aforementioned passages, I'll add both the external and internal verbs as annotations in parenthesis:

"Come to my side, Jane, and let us explain and understand one another." *(COMMAND; **appease**)*

"I will never again come to your side; I am torn away now, and cannot return." *(DENY; **bait**)*

"But, Jane, I summon you as my wife; it is you only I intend to marry." *(PLEAD; **appease**)*

I was silent; I thought he mocked me.

"Come, Jane—come hither." *(COMMAND; **appease**)*

"Your bride stands between us." *(DOUBT; **guilt**)*

He rose, and with a stride reached me.

"My bride is here," he said, again drawing me to him, "because my equal is here, and my likeness. Jane, will you marry me?" *(PERSUADE; **appease**)*

Still I did not answer, and still I writhed myself from his grasp; for I was still incredulous.

"Do you doubt me, Jane?" *(INQUIRE; **discourage**)*

"Entirely." *(DOUBT; **guilt**)*

"You have no faith in me?" *(ENTREAT; **discourage**)*

"Not a whit." *(DOUBT; **guilt**)*

"Am I a liar in your eyes?" *(ENTREAT; **engage**)* he asked, passionately. "Little sceptic, you *shall* be convinced. What love have I for Miss Ingram? None, and that you know. What love has she for me? None, as I have taken pains to prove; I caused a rumor to reach her that my fortune was not a third of what was supposed, and after that I presented myself to see the result; it was coldness both from her and her mother. I would not—I could not—marry Miss Ingram. You—you strange— you almost unearthly thing! I love as my own flesh. You—poor and obscure, and small and plain, as you are *(CONVINCE; **win over**)*—I entreat to accept me as a husband." *(ENTREAT; **win over**)*

"What, me!" I ejaculated, beginning in his earnestness—and especially in his incivility—to credit his sincerity; "me, who have not a friend in the world but you—if you are my friend; not a shilling but what you have given me?" (*DOUBT; self-deprecate*)

"You, Jane. I must have you for my own—entirely my own. Will you be mine? Say yes, quickly." *(BADGER; coerce)*

"Mr. Rochester, let me look at your face; turn to the moonlight." *(EXAMINE; seize)*

"Why?" *(SUPPRESS; stall)*

"Because I want to read your countenance; turn!" *(COMMAND; seize)*

"There you will find it scarcely more legible than a crumpled, scratched page. Read on; only make haste, for I suffer." *(SURRENDER TO; self-deprecate)*

The first external verb we saw in this excerpt with the line *come to my side, Jane, and let us explain and understand one another* was *command*. That works on the surface; Rochester commands Jane to come over. However, he doesn't want to alienate her. Jane has demonstrated her independent mind and will, and she has no actual obligation to stay with him, especially since she plans to leave due to his "impending" nuptials to Blanche Ingram. She refuses with her line: I will never again come to your side; I am torn away now, and cannot return. This line is her attempt to *deny* him the satisfaction of her obedience. An interesting choice for the subtext here is to *bait* him. She wants to know what he'll say, but she does not want to subject herself to his advances. Here, we have a line that works on the simple level of *denying* him, and might not seem to carry with it much subtext. However, there's much more depth here, and examining the line for that depth lets us know we have a conversation that's working—one that moves the story along and yields the depth of character we so ardently desire for our writing.

Rochester then *pleads* with her with his next line: but, Jane, I summon you as my wife; it is you only I intend to marry. However, the subtext is to *appease* her. He recognizes she very well could leave him at that moment, so being straight-forward with his intentions is important to *appease* her potential anxiety. We know this news takes Jane by surprise with the internal description she has here: I was silent; I thought he mocked me. If ever there were a great example of how to weave prose description effectively into strong dialogue, this would be it. The dialogue in this excerpt has such a strong sense of personality that we don't need much description or internal monologue. However, we *do* need a sense of how Rochester's words affect Jane. While we might be able to deduce the effect without this single line of prose description, it helps to clarify her actions and intentions across the rest of the scene, and it does so without **overwriting**, or overexplaining details that were abundantly clear already.

Rochester then *commands* Jane again with the line: come, Jane— come hither; only again, he likely does not want to upset Jane in any way. The subtext here is that he wants to *appease* her. Jane's response is *your bride stands between us*, which casts *doubt* on his intentions; moreover, it *guilts* Rochester for asking such a question, especially if he is indeed betrothed to Blanche, which Jane still believes at this point. We get a prose line here that tells us the blocking: He rose, and with a stride reached me. This little bit allows the reader to understand the subtext of the body language in this moment as well, in addition to his strong intent to get up and move closer to her.

Rochester really cuts to the chase with his next line when he asks: Jane, will you marry me. Perhaps he recognizes Jane does not see his deliberate attempt to make her jealous and fears losing her. Still, *appease* feels like an appropriate verb to describe the subtext here. If you chose or felt something like *mollify* as an appropriate verb, they mean pretty much the same thing, with a slight variety in connotation. That will happen as you apply this exercise. Some verbs will have various shades of meaning that might feel right or better depending on the situation. None of them would be wrong. Jane's silence at this question prompts Rochester to ask his next one: Do you doubt me, Jane? Here, Rochester *inquires* as to Jane's tone, but he also *discourages*

Jane's feelings. Janes response casts *doubt* on Rochester's intentions, but also carries a shade of *guilting* him. This action beat continues on until Rochester is forced to *entreat* Jane with the question: Am I a liar in your eyes? He attempts to *engage* her so he can *convince* and *win her over* with this monologue as a response.

After Rochester asks her to accept him as a husband, Jane asks *what, me?* This question again carries with it the tactic of *doubting* Rochester's intentions, but also with the remainder of the line: me, who have not a friend in the world but you—if you are my friend; not a shilling but what you have given me?, there are undertones of self-deprecation. Jane knows the status of Blanche Ingram and understands she is a more suitable match for Mr. Rochester class-wise. She doesn't yet understand why Mr. Rochester would actually find interest in her as a wife, no matter how much she might actually desire it.

Rochester responds with: You, Jane. I must have you for my own—entirely my own. Will you be mine? Say yes, quickly. On the surface, Rochester brims with that sense of impatience; he *badgers* Jane to say yes. Just below the surface, he *coerces* her to say yes. Problem is, she's not having it. At least not yet. Jane asks to: let me look at your face; turn to the moonlight so that she may *examine* his face. But something else is at play here. Jane is *seizing* control of the situation. She won't say "yes" until she's sure his intentions are sincere.

Rochester attempts to *suppress* her doubts by asking *why?* This line may not carry with it any subtext, so it you thought this line was on-the-nose, I wouldn't say you were wrong. But if we were to attached a more internal verb here, it might be to *stall* Jane because her doubts may be steering her too far away. Jane responds that she *wants to read* his face, and then *commands* him to *turn*. Here again, Jane *seizes* the opportunity. Rochester closes the exchange by *surrendering to* Jane with the analogy in this line: There you will find it scarcely more legible than a crumpled, scratched page. Read on; only make haste, for I suffer. In surrendering to Jane, he *self-deprecates* in the same manner Jane did earlier. The power has completely shifted in the scene, and Jane has seized control. Rochester realizes his attempt at inducing petty jealousy in Jane has failed, and he's at her mercy to requite his advances.

In *Jane Eyre*, often the subtext of the lines of dialogue are so strong, not much prose interference is needed to describe the scene, the emotions, the internal thoughts, the feelings—any of it. Sometimes it's better to let the characters have it out, with simple, unobtrusive descriptions woven in when warranted. Earn these moments. Let the voices of these characters become so strong that any additional prose interference from the author will feel overwritten.

Let's return to our contemporary prose example. As you'll recall, in this scene from Jameson Tabard's darkly comedic novel *The Scottish Bitch*, Cunny Corleone's body has been discovered at the Holy Land Experience, and it has been suspected Latrine Dion has killed her to make it easier for her to win the title in a drag queen competition. Here is the same excerpt, with the prose included:

> Twatla made it to the Holy Land Experiencein under twenty minutes. Duffy speedwalked to intercept her and locked her in a tight embrace.
> "You shouldn't be here."
> Twatla broke free. "That bitch."
> "I know what you're thinking," said Duffy, as if a warning were the next words out of her mouth. "There's no proof yet that Latrine's the one behind this."
> "Just two dead queens who were better than she'll ever be. Isn't that enough?" Twatla noticed there was no crime scene tape. No sign of a body. It must've been taken away.
> Duffy put a hand on her shoulder. "It's just speculation. We don't know enough about Latrine's relationship with either of them, especially Cunny. Look. For all we know it was a hate crime."
> Twatla crossed her arms. "A hate *losing* crime."
> "It could've been Peyton."

"That fucking little murderous leprechaun."

"We can say they're persons of interest. We will investigate them for sure. But that's all we can do right now. They're just not charged with anything." Duffy turned Twatla's face toward hers. "You need to be clear on that."

Now, let's take a look at the same scene with the verbs included in parenthesis.

Twatla made it to the Holy Land Experiencein under twenty minutes. Duffy speedwalked to intercept her and locked her in a tight embrace.

"You shouldn't be here." *(WARN; EMPATHIZE)*

Twatla broke free. "That bitch." *(ACCUSE; DENIGRATE)*

"I know what you're thinking," *(WARN; CALM)* said Duffy, as if a warning were the next words out of her mouth. "There's no proof yet that Latrine's the one behind this." *(WARN; CALM)*

"Just two dead queens who were better than she'll ever be. Isn't that enough?" *(ACCUSE; DENIGRATE)* Twatla noticed there was no crime scene tape. No sign of a body. It must've been taken away.

Duffy put a hand on her shoulder. "It's just speculation. We don't know enough about Latrine's relationship with either of them, especially Cunny. Look. For all we know it was a hate crime." *(MOLLIFY; RATIONALIZE)*

Twatla crossed her arms. "A hate *losing* crime." *(ACCUSE; MOCK)*

"It could've been Peyton." *(DEFLECT; RATIONALIZE)*

"That fucking little murderous leprechaun." *(ACCUSE; MOCK)*

"We can say they're persons of interest. We will investigate them for sure. But that's all we can do right now. They're just not charged with anything." *(MOLLIFY; RATIONALIZE)* Duffy turned Twatla's face toward hers. "You need to be clear on that." *(WARN; COERCE)*

In the opening line of dialogue for the scene, Duffy tells Twatla *you shouldn't be here*, and then proceeds to hug her. The action verb that best describes her tactic with this line of dialogue is to *warn* her—this is an active crime scene, and it's not Twatla's job to be here. However, Duffy knows Twatla has lost one of her dearest friends and fellow drag queens, so the underlying verb here is to *empathize*. If you thought *console* works here as well, I wouldn't say you were wrong. Twatla's response of *that bitch* carries a bold accusation on the surface, but underneath, she intends to put down Latrine—the queen she suspects of committing the crime.

The next two lines of dialogue from Duffy carry the same tactic, despite being separated by the line of prose description. *I know what you're thinking*, and *there's no proof yet that Latrine's the one behind this*, as the prose states, carry the verb *warn* on the surface, but these lines are also attempts to *calm* Twatla. Twatla responds to Duffy with the line *just two dead queens who were better than she'll ever be. Isn't that enough?* Twatla maintains her conviction that Latrine is behind the murders, so her *accusing* remains on the surface, as does her "shady" intention to *denigrate* Latrine in doing so.

Duffy continues to soften the situation for Twatla to calm her, using the tactic *mollify* with the line *It's just speculation. We don't know enough about Latrine's relationship with either of them, especially Cunny. Look. For all we know it was a hate crime.* However, what this line also does is attempt to *rationalize* the situation—to get Twatla to take her emotions out of the situation and look at the crime the way a detective would. Twatla—ever the shady queen that she is—uses the opportunity to throw more shade with her line *A hate* losing *crime*. Here, she maintains her *accusing* mixed with that subtle hint of *mocking* just below the surface. Duffy attempts to *deflect* from the shade and the accusation with the line *it could've been Peyton*. She also maintains the attempt to rationalize the scenario for Twatla. However,

Twatla maintains her same action beat here—she still *accuses* and *mocks* with the line *that fucking little murderous leprechaun.*

Duffy realizes she's not quite getting through to Twatla, so she resumes her tactic of *mollifying* her with that same subtle attempt to *rationalize* the situation for her with the line *We can say they're persons of interest. We will investigate them for sure. But that's all we can do right now. They're just not charged with anything.* Duffy closes this scene with the line *you need to be clear on that.* It's a direct *warning* with a bit more of a sense that she's *coercing* Twatla.

What we're seeing here is that the lines of dialogue, even in prose, need to carry tactics and maintain as much subtext as possible. Performing this process on the dialogue in your manuscript forces you to engage with each line—and subsequently each character—in a productive, detailed manner. For me, this process is vital in ensuring I'm maximizing each character's potential. I examine the tactics, the subtleties, and the dramatic functions of each line of dialogue, and I ask myself the question I've repeated a couple of times in this chapter and the previous one, **what compels this character to speak?** Why not just keep quiet? Why not describe something in the prose?

After I go through the piece and examine the tactics of each line, I return to any lines I recognized as being problematic—those lines with dubious or unclear tactics, perhaps ones that read as too expositional. I consider where I can layer in some of the key components of dialogue with some questions: How can this line carry more conflict? How can this line convey more aspects of character? Can this line imply a little of the theme? Does this line foreshadow something to come?

In Chapters 4 and 5, we will look at the concept of foreshadowing in dialogue more, and we'll consider what to do with those lines that feel really strong despite a lack of subtext.

EXERCISE #5

There are two exercises for this chapter. Let's talk about the first and obvious one: Go through your manuscript, be it novel, short story, screenplay, stage play—whatever, and write out the internal verbs for all of your dialogue. You'll be placing them beside the external action verbs you've already placed, so you can use a different color, font, or style (perhaps ALL CAPS) to distinguish your internal verbs. As with the application of the external verbs, this process is painstaking, but valuable. You are testing the subtext of your lines of dialogue, so you're examining how much depth of character you actually have in each line.

The more you do this exercise, the more likely you are to do the external and the internal verb passes together in one single **dialogue pass**. This is totally okay—whatever works best for you. I find myself doing this quite often with my prose pieces. With screenplays and stage plays, I usually find myself applying this same exercise, but focusing on specific characters because of just how much dialogue there is. I use this exercise to ensure my characters' tactics are consistent and reasonable; therefore, isolating each character to examine their arcs is more productive for me. I call these **character passes.**

In a **character pass**, I go through the entire script and apply this exercise, determining where a character has a tactic change and where the action beats are. Then, I take a break for a bit. Watch a movie. Run errands. Read a book. I return to the script fresh and read the lines for each character separately so I can see the arc, the tactics, and the depth of character. This sometimes means that if I have eight major characters, I'm reading the script eight times, but only focusing on one specific character each time.

EXERCISE #6

The second exercise for this chapter is something you can do in small doses, and it isn't entirely something that's necessary to do. I like to do this for fun after I've gone through the painstaking process of writing the external and internal actions out.

I call this exercise the **hashtag technique**. The hashtag technique applies to the internal actions, or subtext, or the characters, and helps us better understand the hidden intentions of our characters. To do this, we're going to use the hashtag, or # sign, as we would find on social media. The actual function of the hashtag is to aggregate tweets or posts by a specific subject. For example, if I tweet something about the weather in Edinburgh and add #Edinburgh after, then anyone who would like to read tweets pertaining to the city of Edinburgh can type in that hashtag and browse all tweets on that subject. However, the way it's used informally is for social media users to divulge the intended subtext of their tweets. For example, let's look the following tweet:

I just stepped in dog poop in Edinburgh. #livingmybestlife

Obviously, to most people, stepping in dog poop is not living one's best life, so that hashtag is meant to be sarcastic. The tweet's subtext is how much is sucks to step in dog poop. It can even be interpreted that, depending on how much the person likes Edinburgh, even stepping in dog poop in Edinburgh beats stepping in dog poop anywhere else. Either way, the subtext is provided by the hashtag. Let's take a look at this in action with a couple of lines from *Jane Eyre*.

Rochester: You, Jane. I must have you for my own—entirely my own. Will you be mine? Say yes, quickly. #girliwasonlyplaying #cantlivewithoutyou
Jane: Mr. Rochester, let me look at your face; turn to the moonlight. #youthinkthisisfunny #inspectorjaneatwork

Here, the hashtags express the subtext, often in a fun and contemporary way. It's another tool to allow the writer to understand the depth of character and to determine how rich a line of dialogue is. Remember, strong dialogue feels layered and multi-faceted.

To perform this exercise, isolate a dialogue exchange in your work-in-progress. Beside your external and internal verb annotations, write out a few hashtags and play with the hidden intentions of the lines. You may find this exercise to be a fascinating and fun addendum to the process of identifying each line's tactic. I find it allows the line to feel fresh after going through the script or novel a few times. On some occasions, what I write in the hashtag ends up feeling so fresh it better expresses what I wanted the character to say. It can sometimes read funnier, clearer, and more astute than the original line, which absolutely makes the process more worthwhile. Whatever the case, these annotations, including the hashtag exercise, allow you to engage with your dialogue on a more practical level, forcing you to analyze each characters' intentions and how they help shape your story.

CHAPTER 4

CHEKHOV'S GUN

In dramatic writing, the principal of **Chekhov's Gun** is this: "If in the first act you have hung a pistol on the wall, then in the following one it should be fired. Otherwise don't put it there." Here, Russian playwright Anton Chekhov directly states that every part of the play should contribute to the whole. Nothing should feel extraneous. Everything that is set up should pay off. A great example of this is in *Jane Eyre*, when Jane hears strange noises, and a strange, violent attack has occurred against a houseguest named Mr. Mason. Later in the novel, we learn that there is someone unknown (to Jane and other guests) living in the attic. The initial strange sounds and occurrences are **set up** earlier in the novel and **pay off** later. Set ups and payoffs are crucial to your plot, but they're also very useful in dialogue. In fact, they're an element of the **foreshadowing** we discussed earlier in this book.

But how does this work with dialogue? Set ups and payoffs can really add layers and textures to your characters and give the dialogue even more of a sense of subtext. As we saw with the exchange from *Jane Eyre*, Jane is skeptical of Mr. Rochester's proposal to her, so much so, she asks him to turn his cheek so she may study his face. That scene, while pivotal and dramatic, is a payoff to something that was set up a few pages earlier. For Jane to distrust Mr. Rochester, he must have done something to earn her skepticism. Let's look at the exchange that causes the conflict later. This scene **sets up** the scene we examined in Chapter 5.

"Jane," he recommenced as we entered the laurel-walk, and slowly strayed down in the direction of the sunk fence and the horse-chestnut. "Thornfield is a pleasant place in summer, is it not?"

"Yes, sir."

"You must have become in some degree attached to the house—you, who have an eye for natural beauties, and a good deal of the organ of adhesiveness?"

"I am attached to it, indeed."

"And though I don't comprehend how it is, I perceive you have acquired a degree of regard for that foolish little child Adèle, too; and even for simple dame Fairfax?"

"Yes, sir; in different ways, I have an affection for both."

"And would be sorry to part with them?"

"Yes."

"Pity!" he said, and sighed and paused. "It is always the way of events in this life," he continued presently; "no sooner have you got settled in a pleasant resting-place, than a voice calls out to you to rise and move on, for the hour of repose is expired."

"Must I move on, sir?" I asked. "Must I leave Thornfield?"

"I believe you must, Jane. I am sorry, Janet; but I believe, indeed, you must."

This was a blow; but I did not let it prostrate me.

"Well, sir. I shall be ready when the order to march comes."

"It is come now—I must give it to-night."

"Then you are going to be married, sir?"

"Ex-act-ly—pre-cise-ly; with your usual acuteness, you have hit the nail straight on the head."

"Soon, sir?"

"Very soon, my—, that is, Miss Eyre; and you'll remember, Jane, the first time I, or Rumor, plainly intimated to you that it was my intention to put my old bachelor's neck into the sacred noose, to enter into the holy estate of matrimony—to take Miss Ingram to my bosom, in short (she's an extensive armful; but that's not to the point—one can't have too much of such a very excellent thing as my beautiful Blanche)—well, as I was saying—listen to me, Jane! You're not turning your head to look after more moths, are you? That was only a lady-clock [ladybug], child, 'flying away home.' I wish to remind you that it was you who first said to me, with that discretion I respect in you—with that foresight, prudence, and humility which befit your responsible and dependent position—that in case I married Miss Ingram, both you and little Adèle had better trot forthwith. I pass over the sort of slur conveyed in this suggestion on the character of my beloved; indeed, when you are far away, Janet, I'll try to forget it; I shall notice only its wisdom, which is such that I have made it my law of action. Adèle must go to school, and you, Miss Eyre, must get a new situation."

In this passage, though there are clues to Rochester's true intentions with his tone, we see the extent to which Rochester toys with Jane's emotions. At first, it might seem as though the questions had a double meaning, but Jane directly asks Rochester if she should leave Thornfield, and he concurs. Moreover, Rochester directly states he's to be wed to Miss Ingram, so there's no confusion about his attempt to elicit jealousy from Jane. Later in the chapter, when it's clear to Rochester, Jane has taken his words seriously with possibly fleeing to Ireland. She calls him out on his fraudulent behavior with a few lines, one of the most notable being "you play a farce, which I merely laugh at." Rochester realizes he's done more damage by toying with her affections, for if he cannot convince her of his ploy to elicit jealousy, she could very well actually leave.

This example from *Jane Eyre* demonstrates how setting up dialogue earlier can pay off later. It's an element of foreshadowing in that it suggests lines that will come later to respond to the set ups. Additionally, these sets ups and pay offs play an important role in forming the arc of a scene. We begin with information or tactics that are suggested or implied—perhaps obliquely—in dialogue that might seem mundane at first. However, later with **callbacks** or references to these set ups, we see the payoff, further complications, or perhaps even resolution.

Callback lines are perhaps my absolute favorite detail in writing dialogue, and I've found that I seldom have a work in which I haven't used this trope. To me, callback lines are a paradox in that they don't call attention to themselves as being manipulative, but at the same time, they rely on the audience to have remembered a previous line to understand the payoff.

EXERCISE #7

1. Read the short play "Superfan" in the appendix of this book. When you encounter David's line *I don't have change. If you need change, go get some from the Adult Male Fans of My Little Pony booth down the hall*, underline or highlight it. Later, in the play, look for where we have a reference, or **callback** to that line. Underline or highlight that callback line. Think about how that line recalls a previous part of the conversation, yet still pushes the plot forward.

2. In your current Work in Progress (WIP), look to see where you have a line that could function as a set up that you can pay off later. Though this dialogue writing tactic works very well with comedy, it's not limited to that genre. As we've seen with *Jane Eyre*, it works very well with drama also. Sometimes also, a callback line can add a bit of levity to an otherwise heavy drama. Consider injecting a few of these lines into your work. Not only can they add depth of character and foreshadowing, but they can even contribute to the conflict, heightening it in places where the scene might otherwise fall flat. They rely on the audience or reader to recall details, which keeps them both engaged and invested in the story.

CHAPTER 5

ON THE NOSE DIALOGUE

As we've seen with some of the textual examples in previous chapters, good dialogue has layers, and more importantly, subtext. But not every good line has subtext, or even needs it. What happens when we get those lines that say exactly what the character means? Those lines are called **on the nose.** In these lines, characters say exactly what they mean with absolutely no subtext. Now, many script readers and writing instructors might say these lines are to be avoided at all costs, and they're not wrong in preaching that advice. Too many on the nose lines of dialogue leads to boring, bland, unplayable dialogue that sounds stilted or awkward. They are often laughable, and not because they were intended to be so.

In my writing, I follow the mantra that **on the nose** lines of dialogue are not bad, but they must be *earned.* Characters must be pushed or compelled to say exactly what it is they mean—to be as clear as possible—because the circumstances force them to. However, as a general rule, your characters should *imply* what they mean as much as possible, hinting at something they're hiding, *not* getting to the point, and deliberately evading conflict until the conflict compels them to speak clearly.

Let's take a line like "I know you killed my brother," whether it be in a script or a novel. You're correct in thinking this line has no subtext. It doesn't. But does that make it a bad line? Probably not—at least not if this line is the climax of a scene. Perhaps we have two characters who have been avoiding each other at a fancy party, and once they cross paths, they exchange polite conversation that heats until one cannot bear to withhold the truth any further. One guy leans in and says, "I know you killed my brother." This line might then make the blood rush from the accused's face—and perhaps the audience right along with him. A character has been compelled to say exactly what he means, and we're hooked. Compelling the character to speak in an on the nose manner after dancing around the subject piques the audience's interest also. We sit up and take notice, perhaps because we know the truth too, and we're waiting for it to inevitably come out. Earn these on the nose moments in your stories. Create enough tension to force out the clarity.

One of my favorite films to watch for on the nose dialogue is *The Room*, Tommy Wiseau's writing, directing, producing, and acting debut. I would venture to say that ninety-nine percent of the dialogue in this screenplay is on the nose, and that's kind of what makes it both cringeworthy and funny to watch. The dialogue is so stilted and awkward for line after line that there's nothing for the actors to work with—no subtext to play up. Add in some nonsensical plot twists, and you have a mess on your hands. Though this film is by no means anywhere near good, I do encourage viewing at least part of it because it's a great example of what a scene sounds like when every single line is on the nose. It's your example of what *not* to do.

Let's take a look at some earned on the nose lines of dialogue. Let's revisit our attorney story *Molly McDonald, Esquire* and examine a new scene between Molly and Kelly. In this scene, Kelly confronts Molly about her lying and drinking. Molly has said that she's been working late at the office, but Kelly has discovered a receipt from a bar that proves otherwise. Now, the scene could simply get to the point and have the confrontation, but that wouldn't *earn* the on the nose moment of dialogue.

> Molly creeps in through the front door, noticing Kelly sitting on the couch.
>
> MOLLY: You're up. I thought you had to be up early.
>
> KELLY: I do.
>
> MOLLY: Oh, well, it's nice of you to wait up for me then.
>
> KELLY: Another late night at the office?
>
> MOLLY: This case is just... really complicated. All these witnesses.
>
> KELLY: Yeah. I'm sure you've got a lot of evidence to weed through.
>
> MOLLY: Tons.
>
> KELLY: Speaking of evidence, I've got Exhibit A right here.
>
> MOLLY: What do you mean?
>
> Kelly holds out a receipt.
>
> KELLY: You stayed at the office last night working on this case too, right?
>
> MOLLY: Yeah, I... I don't know where you got this.
>
> KELLY: Well, sometimes it's easy to forget that you leave things lying around when you come home after you've been out... working late.
>
> MOLLY: I was working yesterday.
>
> KELLY: Yesterday.
>
> MOLLY: Night. Yesterday night.
>
> KELLY: You were out drinking yesterday night. You stumbled in here, didn't even try to hide it. I heard you throwing up in the bathroom. You have a problem.
>
> MOLLY: I don't know what you're talking about.
>
> KELLY: Molly, be honest about this. For once. For me. For you.

Here, we have a scene where Kelly doesn't quite get right to the point with her goal of getting Molly to admit she has a problem. Her tactic at the beginning is to *prod*. She prods Molly and questions her to tell the truth, waiting to see if Molly will actually take the initiative to admit she has a problem. It would, however, be too easy to get right to the point. But working up to the point where Kelly has boxed Molly in so she has no choice but to admit she has a problem *earns* the direct statement Kelly has at the end. Her line at the end of the scene is entirely on the nose: *You were out drinking yesterday night. You stumbled in here, didn't even try to hide it. I heard you throwing up in the bathroom. You have a problem.* There is no subtext. But because Molly is not taking responsibility for her actions and not confessing to having lied, this line feels appropriate and even climactic. Molly is trapped. This line—and this scene—ends up becoming an **anagnorisis** and perhaps a **peripeteia** moment for Molly. She recognizes her problem and hopefully makes the change to her behavior. This can be a powerful moment in the script.

If this were a film, a complaint might be that perhaps the scene might run a little long. However, the scene isn't *that* long. It's a page of dialogue, and we have enough time to earn that on the nose moment of dialogue without it feeling forced or rushed. However, sometimes in a film, we do cut to a moment with a single line of dialogue that might read as on the nose, lacking subtext completely. I'm not going to say that's wrong as long as that moment is earned. The build up of tension to that moment, even if it's bits of other scenes cut together in a sequence, should earn that moment of on the nose dialogue.

EXERCISE #8

Go back and look at the lines of dialogue where you could not find a subtextual verb to indicate a character's internal goal. Examine if there's no other hidden meaning to the line—no foreshadowing or hint of a theme. This line may be on the nose. If that's the case, examine the arc of your scene and determine if this line has been earned. If this is a film and this line is the only one in the scene, determine if there is enough tension to compel your character to say anything at all. It doesn't have to be an overdramatic reason for speaking, but there should be enough of a reason for this character to utter this line aloud. Perform this test for every line of dialogue you consider to be on the nose. If you don't have enough tension to merit this line, consider cutting it, revising it, or rewriting the scene so the tension builds and compels the character to speak.

CHAPTER 6

SPEECH PATTERNS

THE IMPORTANCE OF GRAMMAR

When I was in graduate school, I took a class in English grammar. Surprisingly, in my all my years of schooling, I'd never officially had a class in English grammar, even as an English major in undergrad. Classes in grammar existed, but they weren't compulsory. They were electives. I didn't know that I really needed to take one. I knew how to use a comma properly; moreover, I knew how to use a semi-colon. What I didn't know was *why* these punctuation marks were important to know. I also discovered that I didn't even know what I didn't know. I didn't know there were sentence patterns. I didn't know there were predicate nominatives. I couldn't explain the difference between a clause and a phrase. I knew instinctively, but I didn't know concretely. Enter one of the most difficult classes I've ever taken. I got an A- in it, and let me tell you, I *worked* for that A-.

I attribute this one difficult grammar class to shaping how I write and giving me the chutzpah to believe that I'm pretty darn good at writing dialogue. Now, I'm not saying every writer needs to take a class in grammar, but I am saying that every writer needs to continue learning every nuance of the language in which they write. The idioms, the phrasing, the word choice—everything—becomes a component of how I have my characters choose to say something. Their own understanding of grammar (or lack thereof) dictates the way they express themselves.

Before I continue, I must reiterate that this is not a book on grammar, nor will this be a chapter exclusively dedicated to basic grammar lessons. This is a chapter on developing your understanding of *how* grammatical choices and rhetorical devices can give your characters and your dialogue something extra special—those quirks that make your characters quotable.

USING SLANG

Using slang in a script or novel can be a tricky thing. For one, it will date your book or film if it is slang specific to a time period. For example, television shows such as *The Brady Bunch* and *Leave it to Beaver* use teenage slang of the era in its dialogue, as do so many of the Beach Party films of the early 1960s. Some of the teen films of the 1980s, like *Sixteen Candles*, *The Breakfast Club*, and *Valley Girl* utilized common turns-of-phrase and this continued into the 90s. Watching these films decades later allows us to see how dated the dialogue is— not that it's such a bad thing. These films were products of their time period and they now feel like wonderful time capsules, and it's not simply because of outdated hairstyles, technology, and fashion. The language of the time period is in the language of its characters.

Some screenwriters have recognized that popular slang of an era dates a film and have created a solution: New, fresh slang just for the characters. Amy Heckerling's *Clueless* invented some slang words for its characters, and the success of the movie actually had a reverse-effect. Instead of being a representation of the generation's slang, it *created* some of its slang. The same can be said for Tina Fey's *Mean Girls*. Everybody—even those who have not seen the film—knows "fetch" will never happen as much as they know who Glen Coco is.

It's worth a shot to develop a form of slang for your characters so they have a specific codified language they use among each other. Or perhaps you want to represent the generation or the town or the time period with a few new slang words. It's worked before. But the key with this choice is that the audience must be able to determine the meaning of the words from the context clues you provide. Simply having your characters throw in made up words or phrases will get confusing. Better yet, make that slang into some form of a joke where another character can mock its use. Regina George did it to Gretchen Wieners in *Mean Girls*. Even the Heathers did it in *Heathers*.

CHARACTER IDIOMS

A specific addition to your arsenal of tricks to improve your characters' dialogue is to give them an idiomatic way of speaking. Give your character a specific phrase or turn-of-phrase that they are known for saying, especially in specific circumstances. This can be a good way to create a memorable line or character quirk and it becomes a good way to address a subtextual aspect of a character's personality.

For example, my family has pointed out to me that I say "Well, that's how it goes" whenever someone says "that's not fair" or when there's a situation that feels like something is unfair. It's basically the same thing as saying "that's life" or "c'est la vie." Word choice can be particularly interesting to play with. Maybe your character has kids, and they've created a language to talk about things in the family. For example, if a toddler gets hurt, maybe you don't call it a "booboo" but an "ow-ee." I know that when my dog licks her paws excessively, I tell her "no lickies," except I say it in a baby voice that comes out as "no wickies."

If your character is multi-lingual, think about how that character might integrate the other language into his or her English. Think about the rules behind that. Perhaps if the character is upset, they swear in another language. Maybe they speak in another language when they don't want the kids to understand what they're saying. My mother and grandmother spoke in Spanish to each other when they didn't want me to understand their discussion. Of course, when I finally learned Spanish, they had to resort to their other language—Tagalog, which I've never quite gotten around to mastering, save for a few key words. That could be a character choice—and a funny one at that. Two characters start speaking in another language, and when a third party overhears, they switch to another.

Think about when to mix the languages and weave them in. For example, being around people who move from Spanish to English in the same sentence my whole life has made me quite adept at the nuances of Spanglish. Maybe your character is stronger in one language, like English and only sprinkles in Spanish for words that are easier to say or more expressive. I once saw an episode of the television show *Happy Endings* where one of the characters spoke fluent Italian only when drinking. Definitely an interesting quirk of character.

DIALECT

Since we're talking about idioms and turns-of-phrase, this is a great place to include a discussion of dialect. Don't confuse giving your characters accents with having them write in a dialect. An accent is defined as a specific pronunciation, usually with people from a given geographical region. A dialect is a speech pattern using different word choices to mean different things, again regarding people from a specific geographical region. The one big tip I can give you here is do **not** write your character's dialogue in an accent. It can get very confusing and it slows down the reader. If it's a screenplay or stage play you're writing, your actors are going to give the character an accent anyway, especially if it's part of the character description. If it's a novel or short story you're writing, your reader will get confused. I used to think this was poor advice. I wrote a novel with one character's dialogue in a specific accent, and it was the number one comment I heard back from agents—nearly unanimously. Cut the accent. Moreover, this was around the time

I sat down to reread the novel *Dracula* by Bram Stoker, and I finally internalized why these agents felt the same way. I love the story, but the sections with heavy accents—where the English words in the dialogue are altered to represent the sounds of the accent—were very difficult to get through. I found those sections much slower to comprehend.

Obviously, there are successful novels where the dialogue is in the accent. Some great titles also include *Their Eyes Were Watching God* by Zora Neale Hurston and *Filth* by Irvine Welsh. Even some plays are written in the accent. *The Iceman Cometh* by Eugene O'Neill uses the older version of the New York accent, replacing the some of the diphthongs with the "oi" sound. For example, *thirty-third street* would become *toity-toid street*. The reader has to sound out the word or say it aloud to understand it better.

There are many other examples to counter my tip, so it's not a hard-and-fast rule. But consider it advice that might alleviate some suffering over responses to your manuscript. I do have a better recommendation: **write in dialect.** Since dialect concerns the word choice and speech patterns of a specific area, you'll still have those regionalisms as markers of authenticity without having to have the accent. This has been a trick I've used for years now, and I love it. It gives me an excuse to travel to the area about which I'm writing and converse with people. I try to take in the general vocabulary, slang, and turns-of-phrase, and it's wonderful to immerse yourself in the culture. Every region has their own dialect, even within the United States.

Let's start there. We all certainly know that *soda* means a carbonated beverage, and many Americans use this word. But Americans in the Midwest call it *pop*. That would be a good marker of a character's background. I grew up calling my shoes *sneakers* only to learn that the rest of the country seems to call them *tennis shoes* (I still can't get the hang of this). Again, that would be imply characters' backgrounds without having to talk about them. In Boston, drinking fountains are called *bubblers*. *Chocolate sprinkles*, the confection we put on ice cream, are called *jimmies*.

The dialect isn't strictly limited to word choice. Speech patterns, or syntax, also can represent a region. In New Jersey, it's common to refer to how long two people have known each other in this way: *I grew up with her. We've known each other since we're twelve.* Note the present tense use of *we are* instead of *we were.* In the South and in Appalachia, *reckon* becomes an interesting case. Adding the word to the start of a sentence also implies the personal pronoun *I.* For example: *Reckon you don't belong in these parts.*

While the United States has several regional expressions and words, it becomes much more apparent in other English-speaking countries. Watch a show like Netflix's *Derry Girls,* and you'll get a Northern Irish dialect so tough to understand for Americans that I've had some friends tell me they had to watch it with the captions on. That's not simply because of the brogue. The word choice is fascinating. For example, several of the girls use the word *cracker* in the same way Americans would say *cool* or *awesome.*

In England, they refer to the *bus* as the *coach.* They refer to a *backpack* as a *rucksack.* They even have some specific syntactical differences. For example, if someone were sent to the hospital (as we'd say it in the United States), in England, they'd say "Johnny is in hospital." Note the elimination of the definite article *the.*

It's extremely important to do your research when writing in dialect, but it lends an authenticity to your characters and implies their backgrounds without having to spoonfeed exposition to your reader or audience. It also lets the reader know, even implicitly, that you've done your homework as a writer.

MY FAVORITE DEVICES

One of the most valuable books I have in my home library is a Dictionary of Rhetorical Devices. These are also sometimes called Dictionaries of Literary Devices. These are handy reference books for finding those interesting and obscure rhetorical devices or flourishes that can give your dialogue and your characters something special. I have a couple of personal rules about using these devices. 1) Use these devices sparingly. These devices are strong, but you don't want your dialogue to be bogged down with too much showy language. 2) Only use these devices if they're in line with something your character would say. If the syntax becomes too intricate for a character who has, say, a high school education, that's an inappropriate use of the device. Refer back to your character profiles and determine if the device fits.

I only like to use devices in my characters' dialogue if they follow the aforementioned rules and if I encounter them enough in my reading to know them innately. You may recognize some of these as well, even if you don't know what they're called.

MALAPROPISM

A malapropism is an incorrect word used that *sounds like* a similar word but isn't exactly the same thing. The resulting effect is usually funny. English playwright Richard Brinsley Sheridan's play *The Rivals* features a character called Mrs. Malaprop, and she often uses this device unknowingly (as is usually the case) in her dialogue. For example, she indicates that one character is at the very "pineapple" of his success. Here, she means *pinnacle*.

Back when I waited tables at a restaurant, I remember walking past the bar in a hurry, and one of the women at the bar turned to me and said, "look at you sautéing past me." After a moment of confusion, I giggled to myself and realized she meant *sauntering*.

Malapropisms can be used for comedic effect, and that's typically the only time you'll see them used. However, consider my aforementioned rules for this. You can really only have one character who does this in your work. Also, don't confuse a malapropism with a pun. A pun is an *intentional* play on words whereas a malapropism is completely unintentional, which brings me to my next favorite device.

PUNS

Puns and witty word play are marks of a more intelligent character and can be used as such. They're also great "Dad Jokes." These devices are quite common, so I won't spend much time on them, but they are wonderful devices to use. They're as common in Shakespeare as they are in *Sex and the City*. I personally love the episode of *Sex and the City* when Carrie Bradshaw attends a baby shower at the home of a friend, and everyone has to remove their shoes at the door. After the shower, her shoes have disappeared, and she holds her friend accountable for their loss. The friend refuses to pay for them because of their exorbitant price (they're Manolo Blahniks), and shames her for frivolously spending money on such an unnecessary thing. The name of this episode? "A Woman's Right to Shoes."

PARAPROSDOKIAN

You've heard this device before. It's when the ending of a statement contradicts its beginning in a surprising way, that leads the listener to have to think about the first part. One funny example is this sentence: "If you've got nothing nice to say about someone, come sit beside me." Another example is by Groucho Marx: "I've had a perfectly wonderful evening, but this wasn't it."

Oscar Wilde uses this device frequently in his plays. For example, in Act II of *An Ideal Husband*: "How pale you are looking Gertrude! It's most becoming." Another example of his from Act II of *A Woman of No Importance* is "I love talking about nothing. It's the only thing I know anything about." Obviously, this is some next-level wittiness and should only be used by those characters who have that level of intelligence and who probably possess a sardonic and wry demeanor. These lines, however, can be magical when used well.

ZEUGMA

Zeugma is the elimination of a word understood to be present still. For example, in the sentence: "She lived upstairs; I down," the missing words lived and -stairs in the second clause are understood to be present. I've used this device in situations where I have a character who needs to run through an explanation of things pretty quickly, and brevity is key to his speech. This device very much calls attention to itself, so using it is a deliberate choice and again, must be done sparingly.

METONYMY

Metonymy is becoming quite common in our slang and everyday language. Metonymy is when something closely associated with a word or name substitutes the actual word or name. For example, *The White House* is metonymy for the Executive Branch of the US government. *The crown* is metonymy for a monarch. Those are more official uses of metonymy, but we start to see this in more slang terms too. *Suits* is metonymy for business executives. *Wheels* is metonymy for *car*. You can easily make up your own examples too that are relevant to your characters and their situations. For example, if your audience or readers are familiar with a group of teenaged students who all take the same high school math class from the same teacher, one character might say, "I got an A in Browning." Here, the characters all understand that this guy got an A in Mrs. Browning's Math class. That's a great use of metonymy because it gives the characters a shared experience and vocabulary. The audience is going to understand its use because the audience knows the students' classes and their teacher.

CONCEIT

A conceit, in a simplistic definition, functions as an extended metaphor. This can be useful if, over the course of a conversation, two or more characters are discussing something that sounds like they're speaking in coded language. For example, in the classic film noir *Double Indemnity*, Barbara Stanwyck's Phyllis Dietrichson and Fred MacMurray's Walter Neff discuss a metaphorical speeding situation. They're actually flirting with each other, and Phyllis warns him that he's moving too fast. The conceit continues for a few lines and provides marvelous word play. In *Mean Girls*, Gretchen Wieners gives a speech to her class on *Julius Caesar* about the relationship between Caesar and Brutus, which is really a conceit about her friendship with Regina George. Conceits can be used in both monologues and dialogue, and they tend to be great for expressing subtext, especially when two people play along with the underlying metaphor.

HYPERBOLE

Hyperbole is an extreme exaggeration, and it's become so commonplace in everyday language that it happens without us even realizing we're doing it. For example, if a new teddy bear wearing a Dr. Who Tardis jacket came out, a Dr. Who fan might say, "take all my money." If someone forgets to turn on their turn signal before turning left, someone might say, "you're literally the worst person in the whole world!" Now, this even exists in emoji form. When something happens that is so funny, I now frequently see people on social media reposting a video with simply a skull as the caption, implying "dead." This means that this video is so funny I've laughed myself to death. We live in a world of hyperbole, and if you have contemporary characters, they will too.

UNDERSTATEMENT

Understatement is deliberately representing something as less than it is to express its magnitude or to downplay its significance. For example, in *Romeo and Juliet*, when Mercutio is mortally wounded, he says it's "just a scratch." A character who might have an immaculately clean house except for a few pieces of mail on the table might apologize and say "excuse the mess" to a houseguest. That line would then suggest a lot about the character, with the inclusion of some context. A character who apologize for a small mess might be a fastidious person or a neat-freak or that character might be passive-aggressively noting that the houseguest's own house is a complete pig sty.

LITOTES

Litotes is a specific form of understatement that states a negative word to affirm a positive. Someone saying "not bad" is a form of litotes. It's also a great, deliberate choice of words for a character. For example, there's a difference between someone referring to someone else as "not ugly" instead of "pretty" or "handsome." That's also a deliberate choice of words. Think about what that line would imply in a given context among a group of women people-watching outside a café.

STICHOMYTHIA

Stichomythia is mostly affiliated with Shakespearean as a device, but we see ancestors of this device in modern films, plays, and novels. Stichomythia is the rapid succession of lines, generally of one sentence each, and in some instances in Shakespeare, one word each. In modern literature and drama, this can be a rapid exchange with just a few words per character. Here's a brief example of what this might look like among modern characters:

Kelly: What the—?
Molly: I can explain.
Kelly: I'm listening.
Molly: It's not—
Kelly: What it looks like.

Stichomythia carries with it a specific rhythm that makes gives dialogue an extra special undertone. The opening of Martin McDonagh's film *In Bruges* begins with the quick patter of stichomythia as Ken (Brendan Gleeson) and Ray (Colin Farrell) discuss how they feel about being in Bruges, Belgium and why they might be there in the first place.

TMESIS

Tmesis, or "cutting" separates a word by inserting another word into it. For example, in the pilot of *Sex and the City*, Carrie Bradshaw asks Mr. Big if he has ever been in love. His response: *Abso-fucking-lutely*. Another common example is when someone exclaims, "unfuckingbelieveable!" Not surprisingly, the use of tmesis tends to include a vulgarity, but it doesn't always have to. A common use of this is the word *nother*. It's obviously not an actual word, but when we say *that's a whole nother story*, the word *another* is cut by the word *whole*.

Tmesis might add some dimension to your character, particularly if they use the former examples with vulgarity. These might be great moments for them, and giving them a word that uses tmesis might be the perfect expression of their feelings in that moment.

This list of devices is by no means exhaustive. You may know or encounter many, many more, and that's wonderful. Think about how your favorite devices might be used by one of your characters and figure out a way to work them in seamlessly, without calling attention to themselves (but ironically still calling attention to themselves). These devices can make your dialogue memorable and compelling and can add layers of complexity. They can add much more depth without having to provide lines of backstory and without having to spoonfeed any indications of their education level. They can imply connection between characters and they can hint at subtext. Have fun with this.

APPENDIX

ADDITIONAL EXERCISES

APPENDIX

OVERVIEW

In this appendix, you'll find the following:

1. The first draft of an original short screenplay. Read this screenplay and afterward, think about how you might alter some of the dialogue. You may even choose to start marking some of the verbs you find and some of the dialogue adjustments as you go.

2. A revision draft of the same screenplay. This will give you the opportunity to flip back to the original script to see what changed.

3. A commentary regarding the revisions on this screenplay. This commentary will explain why I made the changes to the script, with references to some of the lessons and exercises throughout this book.

4. A stage play with which you can practice ascribing action verbs, both internal and external, to the margins.

5. A Glossary

6. A Verb List reference page for checking the tactics of your lines of dialogue.

INT. AMBASSADOR HOTEL LOBBY - DAY

An Ikea-chic lobby. MINDY (30s), a perky sunflower of a woman, clicks on her computer at the reception desk.

> MINDY
> Oh my gosh! My favorite singer in the whole world is staying here tonight. Charisse!

SAM (30s), Mindy's sarcastic friend, checks the computer screen.

> SAM
> That's because she's playing the nearby arena. She needs to stay close by.

> MINDY
> I really hope to meet her. My shift ends at five. I hope she comes to check in before then. Maybe I can call over to the arena and see if they know what time she'll be arriving.

> SAM
> They wouldn't know anything.

ALBIE (50s), their uptight supervisor, marches into the lobby.

> ALBIE
> Mindy. Sam. We have a VIP Guest tonight. Charisse is staying with us after she plays her concert. She plans to check in ahead of time.

                    MINDY
I'm such a big fan.

                    SAM
She really is.

                    ALBIE
I expect you both to remain
professional. Mindy, I'm going
to assign you to be her point
person. That will mean you'll
have to work late tonight.

                    MINDY
Okay, sir. It's not a problem.

                    SAM
I'd like to help too.

                    ALBIE
Fine. Both of you can. But
Mindy, you give Charisse your
work cell number. If there's
anything she needs, you'd
better be on it.

                    MINDY
Yes, sir.

INT. AMBASSADOR HOTEL SUITE - DAY

Mindy supervises the arrangement of a
bouquet of flowers on a table. Sam enters
carrying bags of candy.

                    SAM
Those look pretty.

                    MINDY
Charisse's rider says she
wants fresh cut white lilies.

                    SAM
I got the candy in her rider
too.

                    MINDY
Are those the tropical flavor
ones?

                    SAM
No. Was I supposed to get
those?

                    MINDY
Yes. She doesn't like the
pineapple flavor so we have to
pick them out.

                    SAM
We do? By hand?

                    MINDY
Yes. By hand.

                    SAM
What do you want me to do
with the dried pineapple dog
treats?

                    MINDY
Pineapple? They were supposed
to be sweet potato. No
pineapple anywhere.

                    SAM
          What is wrong with her that
          she doesn't like pineapple?

                    MINDY
          Charisse is my absolute
          favorite singer in the whole
          world. This room has to be
          perfect for her.

                    SAM
          Okay, I understand. I'll go
          exchange these.

                    MINDY
          I'm counting on you.

Mindy takes out another bouquet of lilies
and starts arranging another vase.

INT. AMBASSADOR HOTEL SUITE - NIGHT

The suite is now filled with beautiful
bouquets of flowers, candy organized by
color, plush carpeting, satin pillows, and
ornate draping. Sam trudges into the room,
dragging a shopping bag by her side.

                    SAM
          Here's more incense. I had to
          go to three different stores
          to get it. I smell like dried
          sage now.

                    MINDY
          Doesn't it look great in here?
          This is totally Charisse's
          style. I'm so happy.

                    SAM
She likes a lot of New Agey
things, doesn't she?

                    MINDY
That's her style. Her music
is all about self-care and
loving peace and zen. She's so
inspirational. It makes total
sense that she'd want her
room to look like everything
she sings about. Haven't you
listened to any of her music?

                    SAM
Not really. I know who she is,
but I've never listened to her
music.

                    MINDY
Once we're done with the
potpourri, we'll head down to
the office, and I'll educate
you in all things Charisse. If
we're going to tend to her,
you're going to have to know
everything there is to know
about her.

                    SAM
Then let's get moving. She
should be here soon.

INT. AMBASSADOR HOTEL LOBBY - NIGHT

Mindy and Sam each have an earbud in their
ears, listening to music from Mindy's
phone.

                    MINDY
Don't you just love the

melody? So catchy and exotic.

                    SAM
         Not bad actually. Pretty
         catchy.

Albie sees Mindy and Sam not working and
marches over.

                    ALBIE
         It's not professional to
         listen to music at the front
         desk.

                    MINDY
         Sir, I'm just getting Sam
         caught up on Charisse's music.
         If we're going to attend
         to her every need, we're
         both going to need to know
         everything about her.

                    SAM
         She should be here any minute.

                    ALBIE
         All the more reason for you to
         put it away.

An ENTOURAGE appears, BODYGUARDS clad in
black suits and sunglasses, even despite
its being night and dimly lit. CHARISSE,
a blonde-bombshell of a woman, saunters
in with her hair pulled back and under a
fedora. She also wears dark sunglasses.

Charisse approaches the front desk. Mindy
can barely contain herself.

                    MINDY
          Welcome to the Ambassador
          Hotel, Charisse. We're so
          happy to have you. I'm Mindy,
          and this is Sam. We'll be
          taking care of you today.

Charisse lowers her sunglasses.

                    CHARISSE
          I'd just like my room?

                    MINDY
          Yes, of course. We'll take you
          right up.

INT. AMBASSADOR HOTEL HALLWAY - NIGHT
Mindy, Sam, Charisse, and the entourage
approach Charisse's room.

                    MINDY
          Now, the room is straight
          ahead. Here are six keys for
          you as requested. And... I
          just wanted to say, now that
          my supervisor isn't around...
          I'm a really big fan of yours.

                    CHARISSE
          Thank you.

                    MINDY
          We hope your stay is
          comfortable and that you have
          a great show tonight. If
          there's anything you need,
          please let me or Sam know.

                    CHARISSE
What's your name again?

                     MINDY
     Mindy.

Charisse opens the door and her entourage
files in. The door closes. Mindy and Sam
breathe a sigh of relief. They turn and
start away from the door.

The door opens. Charisse pokes her head
out.

                    CHARISSE
     Mandy?

                     MINDY
     Yes, Charisse?

                    CHARISSE
     I'm supposed to have High
     Mountain Green Tea from China.

Mindy turns to Sam.

                     MINDY
     I thought you said you got the
     green tea.

                      SAM
     I did.

                    CHARISSE
     This is green tea, but it's
     not High Mountain Green Tea.
     It's some cheap substitute

from some Payless kind of
place.

                    SAM
                (sotto voce)
I couldn't find the brand she
wanted anywhere.

                    MINDY
Right away, Charisse. We'll
have it to you as soon as
possible.

                    CHARISSE
I drink it before I go on
stage. I need it before then.

                    MINDY
But you're scheduled to leave
for the arena in less than an
hour.

                    CHARISSE
Get it to me before then.

The door closes. Mindy looks at Sam.

                    MINDY
What are we going to do?

                    SAM
Find some tea and print out a
High Mountain label.

Mindy takes out her phone clicks a button.

                    MINDY

> Find High Mountain Green Tea.

> PHONE
> Search Results for High
> Mountain Green Tea.

Mindy stares aghast at her phone.

> MINDY
> This tea is four hundred
> dollars and it's imported from
> China.

> SAM
> So find some tea and put it in
> a little satchel and give it
> to her.

> MINDY
> At $400 an ounce, I'm sure
> she'll be able to taste the
> quality difference. This is
> Charisse we're talking about
> here.

> SAM
> There's no way we can deliver
> on this in under an hour.

> MINDY
> We have to. It's in her
> contract. We have to try or
> she can sue the hotel. Albie
> will lose his mind. We could
> be fired. It says we can get
> some at the Chinese grocer.
> It's fifteen miles away.

                    SAM
     Is Albie going to let us go?

                    MINDY
     We're supposed to cater to
     Charisse's needs. He has to.

INT. AMBASSADOR HOTEL LOBBY - NIGHT
Albie folds his arms across his chest.

                    ALBIE
     This was supposed to have been
     done already.

                    MINDY
     It's a mistake, sir. But we're
     going to fix it.

                    ALBIE
     I can't front the money for
     this. The money you used was
     all we've gotten from the
     tour. We won't get reimbursed
     for additional expenses for
     another ninety days or so.
     You're going to have to make
     this right.

                    SAM
     Are you saying we should spend
     our own money?

                    ALBIE
     You'll get reimbursed.

                    SAM
     In ninety days.

                        MINDY
          This is for Charisse. I'll
          front the money for it. It's
          my mistake anyway.

                        SAM
          Mindy.

                        MINDY
          No. We're going to do this
          right. She'll notice how hard
          we're working. She'll find a
          way to reward us. I know it.

EXT. MINDY'S CAR - NIGHT
Mindy's car is stuck in traffic.

INT. MINDY'S CAR - NIGHT
Mindy grips the steering wheel. Sweat
drips from her brow.

                        SAM
          We're never going to make it
          back to the hotel. We're going
          to have to meet her at the
          arena.

                        MINDY
          Okay. We can do that. She just
          said she drinks it before she
          goes on stage.

Mindy touches her stomach.

                        SAM
          Are you okay?

                    MINDY
My stomach really hurts.
Happens every time I get
stressed.

                    SAM
This isn't worth it. You're
worrying yourself sick. Let's
call it a night and head home.

                    MINDY
No. Charisse needs this, and
I spent half my rent money on
it. We're going to give it to
her.

EXT. REAR OF ARENA - NIGHT
Mindy parks her car and scrambles out. She
and Sam run between tour busses that are
parked outside.

                    MINDY
Come on. We can do this.

EXT. ARENA DOOR - NIGHT
A BODYGUARD stops Mindy and Sam.

                    BODYGUARD
You need a credential to get
in.

                    MINDY
We don't have a credential.
We're Mindy and Sam from the
Ambassador Hotel. We saw you
earlier.

                    BODYGUARD
          I don't remember you.

                    MINDY
          From the lobby. With Charisse.
          You're one of her bodyguards.

                    SAM
          I have my Ambassador ID.

                    BODYGUARD
          No fans allowed.

                    SAM
          We're not fans.

                    MINDY
          Well, we are. But Charisse
          sent us to get some tea. High
          Mountain Green Tea imported
          from China. She said she needs
          it before she gets on stage.

The Bodyguard speaks into his wrist to
verify. Mindy and Sam stare at each other
nervously. Mindy clenches her stomach.

                    SAM
          You okay?

                    MINDY
          I'll be fine.

The Bodyguard motions them through.

INT. ARENA HALLWAY - NIGHT

Mindy and Sam run down the hallway.

>   MINDY
> She goes on in half an hour.

INT. ARENA BACKSTAGE AREA - DAY

Mindy and Sam slow down as they enter the immaculate backstage area, that completely resembles the suite Mindy put together for Charisse.

>   SAM
> Well, you definitely nailed
> the room decorating.

>   MINDY
> It's so wonderful.

Mindy clenches her stomach.

>   SAM
> You okay?

>   MINDY
> I'll be fine. There she is.

Mindy and Sam approach Charisse.

>   MINDY (CONT'D)
> Excuse me, Charisse? We have
> your High Mountain Green Tea
> just in time. You can drink it
> before you have to go onstage.

Charisse takes the bag and throws it at Mindy.

                    CHARISSE
          I'm supposed to drink it
          before I leave the hotel.
          Thanks for ruining my show,
          Mandy.

                    SAM
          Now listen to me, Charisse--

Mindy grabs her stomach and projectile
vomits all over Charisse. Mindy is
horrified at first. Then, she takes pride
in what happened.

                    MINDY
          My name is Mindy.

Mindy and Sam turn and saunter away from
Charisse. Sam puts her arm around Mindy.

                              FADE TO BLACK

THE AMBASSADOR REVISIONS COMMENTARY

The initial screenplay for "The Ambassador" had a relatively solid structure, so the revisions on which I focused were squarely on dialogue revision. This commentary will help explain these revisions with a little more detail beyond markings on the page.

The opening line spoken by Mindy gives away too much information, which is a significant problem for much of this script's dialogue. I chose to delay revealing that Charisse is Mindy's "favorite singer in the world" until a few lines later. This way, she can engage with Sam a little more. It also gives her a great surface action with the line—to verify that what she's reading is right. Moreover, Sam gets to respond with""Makes sense. She's performing nearby." The audience learns more information here, and Sam *clarifies* and *verifies* that what Mindy says is correct. The next line is when Mindy reveals her Charisse fandom, and in keeping with this tactic of *questioning* and *verifying*, we're keeping the conversation moving as well as revealing more information. This technique avoids the information dump, yet still subtly reveals important details to the audience that will set up later conflicts.

Albie's first line was a little too wordy in the first draft, so cutting it down made his subtext tactic of *warning* a little stronger here. Having Mindy overreact and having her apologize works in the revision because

Albie has already implied that Charisse is someone to be handled with care. Sam's retort gives us more insight into Sam's characterization and reveals how little Sam knows about Charisse in the following line: "Apparently. Moving the expectation portion of Albie's line to the end with "I hope I don't have to remind you of your professionalism with VIPs" really emphasizes that *warning* tactic Albie employs.

If Sam doesn't know too much about Charisse, then it wouldn't make sense for her to offer to help. Having Mindy's enthusiasm carry through the next line forces Sam into the plot and is more logical; Sam would have no reason to volunteer otherwise. Mindy's volunteering her provides an opportunity for some comedy, especially since the subtext in Sam's line "I don't know her" is to *decline*.

Always look for redundancy in your dialogue. We have a great example of that in Albie's line "Fine. Both of you can." Simply saying "fine" already implies that he's allowing them both to work the VIP hospitality. Mindy's *reassurance* in the last line of the scene becomes really important then, especially since it now seems Sam is an unwilling participant in this adventure.

In the second scene, I changed Sam's line from "I got the candy in her rider too" to "so here's the candy." This change implies a little more attitude for Sam, and we didn't need to hear Sam repeat the word "rider" since Mindy had just said it in the previous line. In Mindy's third line in the scene, I added "when you get back" to indicate when they'd be picking out the pineapple flavored candy for Mindy to imply that Sam is going to have to go back out and get the right candy. There are some minor changes in the ensuing lines to improve the flow of the scene—mostly transitions. I did change the very on the nose line "Charisse is my absolute favorite singer in the whole world. This room has to be perfect for her." The line has no subtext and there's little for the actor playing Mindy to do with this line. The new line implies that Mindy *worships* Charisse and follows her on social media. This detail gives more dimension to Mindy's characterization, and by default—Charisse.

In Sam's response—her last line in the scene—I cut the words "I understand." These words are already implied, so they're redundant. Keeping the mantra of "less is more" with dialogue, Sam's line is shorter and sweeter here.

In Scene Three, I did add the action *Mindy admires the room* to provide some given imagery to support Mindy's first line in the scene better—her response to Sam. Many of the lines of dialogue in this scene have been combined. Sam would be more likely to divulge her experience and assumptions about Charisse earlier and up front in the scene. With Mindy's last line, however, I did change the order of the sentences. What was the last sentence "if we're going to tend to her, you're going to have to know everything there is to know about her" has become the first line of the dialogue. Adding the bit about the "crash course in Charisse 101" gives Mindy more of a personality in her dialogue and gives us some insight into how she talks to her friends.

In Scene 4, I preferred Sam's starting us off and giving us her take on Charisse's music. There was an implied question about how Sam would like her music at the end of Scene 3, and giving Sam the first line as a reaction helps to answer it. I cut the sentence "I'm just getting caught up on Charisse's music" because the audience already knows this, and Mindy's next sentence already implies what she's doing, especially if she's going to *defend* her action of listening to music at the reception desk. The rest of the scene remains the same. Giving Charisse such a grand entrance as well as a curt first line really tells us Charisse treats employees as expendable and inferior.

For Mindy's interaction with Charisse in Scene 5, it's important to have her gush a bit, but in a way that wouldn't be as direct as "I'm a really big fan of yours." It's not that it's a bad line, but the line is on the nose and doesn't imply enough about Mindy. Adding that she "listens to [her] albums on a loop" and that Charisse is Mindy's "mantra" gives us more of the impact of Charisse on Mindy.

I did change Charisse's line "I'm supposed to have High Mountain Green Tea from China" to "my rider says" more so because this adds a throwback to Mindy's conversation with Sam earlier about Charisse's rider. There's a bit of a pay off now to the line that was set up earlier. Where Charisse clarifies that the tea Mindy and Sam got was "some off-brand generic tea from some drug store checkout line," the original line worked better in my opinion. However, I did change it to avoid the specific brand "Payless." I also simplified Charisse's next line from "I drink it before I go on stage. I need it before then" to "I need it before I go on stage." The reasoning is that Charisse needs to be as direct as possible, and using fewer words sharpens the impact on Mindy and Sam here.

Mindy's line "This tea is four hundred dollars" has more of an impact just leaving it as that sentence, cutting the clause "and it's imported from China." The audience already knows that; Charisse mentioned it already. I liked the idea of adding "at the Bargain Bin" to Sam's line because it *undermines* everything Charisse said, and it tells us more of how Sam feels about Charisse. She's over her and all of this. Simplifying Mindy's response to "She's gonna know the difference. She's Charisse" really helps get to the point. Moreover, we already know it's four hundred dollars an ounce, and it's implied that she'd be able to taste the difference in quality because "she's Charisse." That short sentence already says so much because we know Mindy has praised Charisse's style and taste.

After simplifying Mindy's next line, I changed the direction of the next scene by changing Sam's direct question from "Is Albie going to let us go?" to "Is Albie going to give us more money?" That's an important change because it sharpens the point of the following scene: that Mindy and Sam will have to use their own money.

In Scene 6, the confrontation with Albie, I did cut Albie's first line because it's already implied that they were supposed to have gotten the tea for Charisse. Starting the scene on Mindy's line "It's a mistake, sir. But we're going to fix it" has more impact because it implies that Albie has already *scolded* them, forcing Mindy to *apologize*. I cut the first sentence of Albie's response to Mindy's apology because it's already implied that Albie "can't front the money." Eliminating redundancies like this are a big part of the dialogue revision process. It creates the opportunity for more subtext and doesn't feel like you're spoonfeeding information to the audience.

The rest of the scene has some minor alterations to make some of the dialogue more concise. I did like the idea of ending the scene with Mindy's reminding Sam of Charisse's gratitude philosophy, and ending with a sarcastic remark from Sam both *undermines* Mindy's optimism and *foreshadows* the ending of the film.

Scene 7 is the establishing shot of their driving in the car in heavy traffic with no dialogue. Much of the dialogue revision in Scene 8 was about improving the concision. Since there's an urgency to the girls' goals at this point, their being long-winded works against their goals. Keeping the dialogue as concise as possible in this scene was paramount. For example, Sam's original opening line began with the sentence "We're never going to make it back to the hotel." We already know this information because the next line about meeting her at the arena implies that they don't have time to get back to the hotel first. This revision is an example of cutting dialogue for concision. You'll notice that the rest of the dialogue is cut down for this reason—finding places where there's redundancy and allowing the urgency of the scene to dictate the bare-bones information needed here. I did add Sam's sentence "Nobody's worth getting sick over" for a couple of reasons. Firstly, it implies that Sam is very much over Charisse. Secondly, it really emphasizes Mindy's stomach problems to provide a proper set up for the denouement of the film.

Scene 9 has that one line of dialogue as they park and head inside. At the start of Scene 10, remembering that film is a visual medium, I liked the idea of the Bodyguard holding up his badge and gesturing to it rather than the direct spoken question about security badges. Eliminating the line becomes much more effective here, allowing the visuals to speak more—especially since Mindy also mentions the credential in her first line of the scene.

Scene 11 is the scene of Sam and Mindy running down the hallway. Scene 12 originally began with Sam's line, "Well, you definitely nailed the room decorating." I felt like this was a great opportunity for some wry sarcasm—something short and sweet. I changed her line to "Well, this is yoga-tastic." I also cut Mindy's next line because her saying it was all "wonderful" undercut her stomach anxiety as well as her changing feelings about how Charisse has been treating her.

Charisse's last line needed to sound much more petulant and spoiled, so I changed some of the verbiage. Moreover, I did want to emphasize the gratitude motif and theme here, especially since the reason Mindy reveres Charisse so much is for her positivity. It turns out Charisse's positivity is laced with passive aggression. Not so positive after all.

I changed Sam's first line from the more cliché, "now listen to me" to "first of all" because the latter implies that Sam has a long tirade coming where she's going to enumerate all of Charisse's wrongs. Of course, that's cut short by Mindy's projectile vomit.

A big theme in this film revolves around the topic of gratitude and is expressed thematically as "true gratitude comes from the heart" and "gratitude must be shown more than uttered." Another theme is the idea that meeting your idols can sometimes be disappointing; they're never going to live up to the mythic qualities you may have ascribed to them. All of the dialogue and actions in this script—and later, the way the film would be shot and the way it would sound—should help to convey these themes. Knowing what the script or story is trying to say really helps guide the revision process, so make sure that the themes and motifs are clear before you embark on the revision journey. And if they're not clear, that's okay. Going through this process may help the themes crystallize for you.

INT. AMBASSADOR HOTEL LOBBY - DAY

An Ikea-chic lobby. MINDY (30s), a perky sunflower of a woman, clicks on her computer at the reception desk.

              MINDY
     Is this for real? Charisse is
     staying here?

SAM (30s), Mindy's sarcastic friend, checks the computer screen.

              SAM
     Makes sense. She's performing
     nearby.

              MINDY
     Do you think she'll check in
     before five? That's when I
     get off, and I'm like... her
     biggest fan. Maybe I can call
     the arena.

              SAM
     How would they know anything?

ALBIE (50s), their uptight supervisor, marches into the lobby.

              ALBIE
     Mindy. Sam. We have a VIP
     Guest tonight. Charisse plans
     to check in before she plays
     her concert.

                    MINDY
     Score! Sorry. I'm a huge fan.

                    SAM
     Apparently.

                    ALBIE
     I hope I don't have to remind
     you of your professionalism
     with VIPs, Mindy. I'm going
     to assign you to be her point
     person. That'll mean you'll
     have to work late tonight.

                    MINDY
     Of course not, Sir. But can
     Sam help?

                    SAM
     Me?

                    ALBIE
     Fine. But Mindy, you give
     Charisse your work cell
     number. If there's anything
     she needs, you'd better be on
     it.

                    MINDY
     Yes, sir. Sam, you're gonna
     love her.

INT. AMBASSADOR HOTEL SUITE - DAY
Mindy supervises the arrangement of a

bouquet of flowers on a table. Sam enters
carrying bags of candy.

                    SAM
        Those look pretty.

                    MINDY
        Charisse's rider says she
        wants fresh cut white lilies.

                    SAM
        So here's the candy.

                    MINDY
        Are those the tropical flavor
        ones?

                    SAM
        No. Was I supposed to get
        those?

                    MINDY
        Yes. But she doesn't like the
        pineapple flavor so we have
        to pick them out when you get
        back.

                    SAM
        We do? By hand?

                    MINDY
        Yes. By hand.

                    SAM
        Then, what do you want me to
        do with the dried pineapple
        dog treats?

                    MINDY
        Pineapple? They were supposed
        to be sweet potato. No
        pineapple anywhere.

                    SAM
        What is wrong with her that
        she doesn't like pineapple?

                    MINDY
        She's a goddess with
        impeccable taste. Have you
        seen her social media? She'll
        post about it. It has to be
        perfect.

                    SAM
        Okay, okay. I'll go exchange
        these.

                    MINDY
        I'm counting on you.

Mindy takes out another bouquet of lilies
and starts arranging another vase.

INT. AMBASSADOR HOTEL SUITE - NIGHT
The suite is now filled with beautiful
bouquets of flowers, candy organized by

color, plush carpeting, satin pillows, and ornate draping. Sam trudges into the room, dragging a shopping bag by her side. Mindy admires the room.

> SAM
>
> Here's more incense. I had to go to three different stores to get it. I smell like dried sage now. She likes a lot of New Agey things, doesn't she?

> MINDY
>
> That's her style. Her music is all self-care. Peace. Love. Zen. It makes total sense that she'd want her room to look like everything she sings about. Haven't you listened to any of her music?

> SAM
>
> I mean, I know who she is, but no.

> MINDY
>
> If we're going to tend to her, you're going to have to know everything there is to know about her. Once we're done with the potpourri, we'll head down to the office, and I'll give you a crash course in Charisse 101.

                    SAM
         Then let's get moving. She
         should be here soon.

INT. AMBASSADOR HOTEL LOBBY - NIGHT

Mindy and Sam each have an earbud in their
ears, listening to music from Mindy's
phone.

                    SAM
         Not bad actually. Pretty
         catchy.

                    MINDY
         So catchy and exotic.

Albie sees Mindy and Sam not working and
marches over.

                    ALBIE
         It's not professional to
         listen to music at the front
         desk.

                    MINDY
         Sir, if we're going to attend
         to her every need, we're
         both going to need to know
         everything about her. Sam's
         been living in a bubble.

                    SAM
         She should be here any minute.

                    ALBIE
        All the more reason for you to
        put it away.

An ENTOURAGE appears, BODYGUARDS clad in
black suits and sunglasses, even despite
its being night and dimly lit. CHARISSE,
a blonde-bombshell of a woman, saunters
in with her hair pulled back and under a
fedora. She also wears dark sunglasses.

Charisse approaches the front desk. Mindy
can barely contain herself.

                    MINDY
        Welcome to the Ambassador
        Hotel, Charisse. We're so
        happy to have you. I'm Mindy,
        and this is Sam. We'll be
        taking care of you today.

Charisse lowers her sunglasses.

                    CHARISSE
        My room?

                    MINDY
        Yes, of course. We'll take you
        right up.

INT. AMBASSADOR HOTEL HALLWAY - NIGHT

Mindy, Sam, Charisse, and the entourage
approach Charisse's room.

                    MINDY
          Now, the room is straight
          ahead. Here are six keys for
          you as requested. And... I
          just wanted to say, now that
          my supervisor isn't around...
          I listen to your albums like,
          on a loop. You're my mantra.

                    CHARISSE
          Thank you.

                    MINDY
          We hope your stay is
          comfortable and that you have
          a great show tonight. If
          there's anything you need,
          please let me or Sam know.

                    CHARISSE
          What's your name again?

                    MINDY
          Mindy.

Charisse opens the door and her entourage
files in. The door closes. Mindy and Sam
breathe a sigh of relief. They turn and
start away from the door.

The door opens. Charisse pokes her head
out.

                    CHARISSE
          Mandy?

                    MINDY
Yes, Charisse?

                  CHARISSE
My rider says High Mountain
Green Tea from China.

Mindy turns to Sam.

                    MINDY
I thought you said you got the
green tea.

                    SAM
I did.

                  CHARISSE
This is green tea, but it's
not High Mountain Green Tea.
It's off-brand generic garbage
from some drug store checkout
line.

                    SAM
            (sotto voce)
I couldn't find the brand she
wanted anywhere.

                    MINDY
Right away, Charisse. We'll
have it to you as soon as
possible.

                  CHARISSE
I need it before I go on stage.

                    MINDY
          But you're scheduled to leave
          for the arena in less than an
          hour.

                    CHARISSE
          Get it to me before then.

The door closes. Mindy looks at Sam.

                    MINDY
          What are we going to do?

                    SAM
          Find some tea and print out a
          High Mountain label.

Mindy takes out her phone clicks a button.

                    MINDY
          Find High Mountain Green Tea.

                    PHONE
          Search Results for High
          Mountain Green Tea.

Mindy stares aghast at her phone.

                    MINDY
          This tea is four hundred
          dollars.

                    SAM
So find some tea at the
Bargain Bin and put it in a
little satchel and give it to
her.

                    MINDY
She's gonna know the
difference. She's Charisse.

                    SAM
There's no way we can deliver
on this in under an hour.

                    MINDY
We have to. It's in her
contract. She could sue the
hotel. Albie will lose his
mind. We could be fired. Look,
they have it at the Chinese
grocer. It's fifteen miles
away.

                    SAM
Is Albie going to give us more
money?

                    MINDY
We're supposed to cater to
Charisse's needs. He has to.

INT. AMBASSADOR HOTEL LOBBY - NIGHT
Albie folds his arms across his chest.

                    MINDY
It's a mistake, sir. But we're
going to fix it.

                    ALBIE
The money you used was all
we've gotten from the tour.
We won't get reimbursed for
additional expenses for
another ninety days or so. We
don't have $400 in petty cash.
You're going to have to make
this right.

                    SAM
So we use our own money?

                    ALBIE
You'll get reimbursed.

                    SAM
In ninety days.

                    MINDY
This is for Charisse. I'll
front the money for it. It's
my mistake anyway.

                    SAM
Mindy.

                    MINDY
No. We're going to do this
right. She'll notice how hard
we're working. Knowing her,

she will be grateful. She has
a whole song about gratitude.

                SAM
Is the title "Expensive Tea?"

EXT. MINDY'S CAR - NIGHT
Mindy's car is stuck in traffic.

INT. MINDY'S CAR - NIGHT
Mindy grips the steering wheel. Sweat
drips from her brow.

                SAM
We're going to have to meet
her at the arena. There's no
time.

                MINDY
She just said she drinks it
before she goes on stage.

Mindy touches her stomach.

            MINDY (CONT'D)
My stomach really hurts.
Happens every time I get
stressed.

                SAM
Nobody's worth getting sick
over. Let's call it a night
and head home.

                    MINDY
          No. Charisse needs this, and
          I spent half my rent money on
          it. We're going to give it to
          her.

EXT. REAR OF ARENA - NIGHT

Mindy parks her car and scrambles out. She
and Sam run between tour busses that are
parked outside.

                    MINDY
          Come on. We can do this.

EXT. ARENA DOOR - NIGHT

A BODYGUARD stops Mindy and Sam. He
gestures for them to flash their badges.

                    MINDY
          We don't have a credential.
          We're Mindy and Sam from the
          Ambassador Hotel. We saw you
          earlier.

                    BODYGUARD
          I don't remember you.

                    MINDY
          From the lobby. With Charisse.
          You're one of her bodyguards.

                    SAM
          I have my Ambassador ID.

                    BODYGUARD
No fans allowed.

                    SAM
We're not fans.

                    MINDY
Well, we are. But Charisse
sent us to get some tea. High
Mountain Green Tea imported
from China. She said she needs
it before she gets on stage.

The Bodyguard speaks into his wrist to
verify. Mindy and Sam stare at each other
nervously. Mindy clenches her stomach.

                    SAM
You okay?

                    MINDY
I'll be fine.

The Bodyguard motions them through.

INT. ARENA HALLWAY - NIGHT
Mindy and Sam run down the hallway.

                    MINDY
She goes on in half an hour.

INT. ARENA BACKSTAGE AREA - DAY
Mindy and Sam slow down as they enter the
immaculate backstage area, that completely

resembles the suite Mindy put together for
Charisse.

                    SAM
          Well, this is yoga-tastic.

Mindy clenches her stomach.

                    SAM (CONT'D)
          You okay?

                    MINDY
          I'll be fine. There she is.

Mindy and Sam approach Charisse.

                    MINDY (CONT'D)
          Excuse me, Charisse? We have
          your High Mountain Green Tea
          just in time. You can drink it
          before you have to go onstage.

Charisse takes the bag and throws it at
Mindy.

                    CHARISSE
          I wanted it before I left the
          hotel. Thanks for ruining my
          show, Mandy.

                    SAM
          First of all--

Mindy grabs her stomach and projectile

vomits all over Charisse. Mindy is
horrified at first. Then, she takes pride
in what happened.

                    MINDY
         My name is Mindy.

Mindy and Sam turn and saunter away from
Charisse. Sam puts her arm around Mindy.

                         FADE TO BLACK

Character Name	Brief Description	Age	Gender
FABIAN	Skinny super-nerd, socially awkward	20s	M
DAVID	Has-been actor, speaks w/ affectation	40s	M
BRANDY	Sexy, bordering on slutty	20s-30s	F
ANNOUNCER	Recording	N/A	M/F

*Note: "Cisor" is pronounced "Size-or"

FADE UP:

(A simple table and chair. On the table is a black sharpie with some headshots and/or promotional photos. Beside the table is an easel with a poster that reads 2pm: David Amesbury: The Cisor. Stage right is a queue with one single fan: FABIAN. FABIAN, a twenty-something nerdy superfan wears a t-shirt with the "Cisor" logo, angel wings on his back constructed of wire hangers, and a halo made of gold garland. He holds an autograph book and pen, eagerly awaiting his idol. An ANNOUNCEMENT can be heard.)

ANNOUNCEMENT

Attention Mega-Hero Con: Please join every body's favorite superhero from 90s basic cable in the Magnolia Room off the Grand Concourse. Don't miss y our chance to meet the Cisor himself, David Amesbury.

(DAVID motions for FABIAN to approach the table. FABIAN runs up.)

FABIAN

Wow. I can't believe it! David Amesbury. Can I call you Cisor?

(DAVID gets right to signing an autographed picture.)

DAVID

You can call me M r. Amesbury.

FABIAN

Okay. Right. Of course. Mr. Amesbury . I'd love it if you could make out with me. I mean, make it out to me. Fabian. I'm Fabian.

DAVID

Autographs are thirty dollars. Cash only.

(FABIAN digs in his pocket and puts the cash on the table.)

DAVID

I don't have change. If you need change, go get some from the Adult M ale Fans of My Little Pony booth down the hall.

FABIAN

You can keep the change, sir. The Bronies are a bunch of bullies.

DAVID

Now that's F-A-

FABIAN

B.

DAVID

B. Yes, of course.

FABIAN

I-A-N. I'm Fab-Ian.

DAVID

I'm sure you are.

(DAVID hands the picture to FABIAN.)

FABIAN

And, Mr. Amesbury, sir. Could you just write me a message in my autograph book? I've already had messages from Spiderman and Superman and Batman and Wonder Woman and--

DAVID

An additional autograph will be another thirty dollars.

FABIAN
Yes, sir.

(FABIAN drops more cash on the table. DAVID motions for him to fork over the autograph book.)

FABIAN

Could you just write what you always said in every episode?

DAVID

How about if I just sign my name again?

(FABIAN is disappointed, but he doesn't want to seem that way.)

FABIAN

Right. Yes. Of course. You are the Cisor. The Cisor-meister. The super-warrior. Half- man, half-angel, the most noble of all the Avians. How could I ask for anything more?

DAVID

Precisely.

FABIAN

Could you just say it for me then?

DAVID

I really can't. Copyright laws and such.

FABIAN

But I'm your biggest fan. It really--It would mean the world to me.

DAVID

No, I can't, you see. I have other fans waiting for me.

FABIAN

Right. Yes. You are right. You have other fans. I'm so rude taking up all your time.

DAVID

Thank you. See? Here's one now.

(FABIAN steps aside. Both of their heads follow from right to left. DAVID looks disappointed.)

FABIAN

I think he was a Bronie, sir. So, remember that one time in season two, episode six, how you were summoned by the King of the Avians to defeat the evil Slaghorns of Wicked Canyon?

DAVID

Vaguely.

FABIAN

I was in that episode. I was an extra. I won a sweep stakes on the back of the Cisor cereal box. Remember how you had that cereal?

DAVID

I'd rather forget.

FABIAN

It was so yummers in my tummers. I ate it every day for three years.

DAVID

It was discontinued after two months. The marshmallows had lead contamination.

FABIAN

I bought it in bulk. I love the taste of pencils.

DAVID

That explains a lot.

FABIAN

So in the episode, I got to play one of the Avians who come to y our aid.

DAVID

I'm sure you did a lovely job, but really, I have other fans to attend to.

FABIAN

Right. There I go again. Being rude. Sorry, Mr. Amesbury.

(FABIAN step s aside again for not even a half-beat before going back into his story.)

FABIAN

So anyway, after you enlisted the help of the Avians, the evil Slaghorns attacked your army. I was the first guy they killed. The evil Slaghorns pushed me into Wicked Canyon. I got to do a stunt! It was such mega-cooly -coolness. I even broke my arm. The Slaghorns really made you angry. You were so mad when y ou saw me get pushed that you got up on the edge of the rocky cliff and said--

DAVID

I'm not going to say it, Franklin.

FABIAN

Fabian, sir. It was such a great moment. It's the moment that made me a man.

DAVID

Just when I thought lead had stunted your growth.

FABIAN

Come on, Mr. Amesbury. Please say it.

DAVID

Did you know I played the Duke of Buckingham in Richard the Third? Huh? Did you see me as Coriolanus at the Green Hills Playhouse? What about my role as Orestes in the Sidewalk Theatre performance of Electra, a role that the Citrus Grove Gazette called "fit for an actor?"

FABIAN

I remember when you were on Letterman. Remember that time? That time you were on Letterman? He made you get up on his desk to say it. Huh? Remember? Since you said it for him, could you say it for me?

(BRANDY APPLE enters the queue, wearing devil horns, bat-wings made of wire hangers, and a dominatrix-esque skirt. She holds a plastic pitchfork and approaches the table. DAVID is spellbound.)

DAVID

Sweet Mary of Magdalene.

FABIAN

No, that wasn't it. You said--

(FABIAN turns around and sees her.)

DAVID

Can I help you? Step aside, Farnsworth.

FABIAN

Fabian.

BRANDY

Mr. Amesbury, I'm your biggest fan.

DAVID

Please, call me David. Or Cisor. Or anything you'd like, really.

FABIAN

But I'm your biggest fan, Mr. Amesbury.

BRANDY

I own every episode on Blu-Ray.

DAVID
(To BRANDY)

Do you?

FABIAN

I do too.

BRANDY

You are so much more handsome in person.

DAVID

Am I?

FABIAN

And he has so many more fans waiting for him, right M r. Amesbury?

DAVID

Go lick a pencil, Florence.

BRANDY

Could you give me your autograph?

DAVID

I'd be glad to.

(DAVID begins to sign a headshot.)

BRANDY

Oh no. Not that. Do me.

(BRANDY pushes up the top of her breast.)

FABIAN

He doesn't do that sort of thing. He's the noble Cisor.

BRANDY

Or you could sign my Wicked Canyon.

FABIAN

He only goes to Wicked Canyon to drive out the Slaghorns.

BRANDY

There are a lot of Slaghorns in my Wicked Canyon.

(BRANDY's face is mere inches from DAVID's, their eyes locked.)

FABIAN

Okay, lots of fans waiting for you, Mr. Amesbury.

DAVID

Tell them I'm busy. To whom should I make the autograph out?

BRANDY

My name is Brandy Apple.

FABIAN

Ew.

DAVID

Delicious.

                    FABIAN
He charges thirty dollars. Cash only.

                    BRANDY
I'm only in town to see you.

                    DAVID
No charge. So tell me, what do you do when you're not dressed as a
temptress?

                    BRANDY
I'm in the movie business.

                    DAVID
Are you a fellow thespian?

                    BRANDY
Something like that.

                    FABIAN
She sounds fishy, Mr. Amesbury. I will be your dutiful squire and
google her.

          (FABIAN whips out his phone.)

                    DAVID
What are you working on now?

                    BRANDY
I'm doing a film where I play Cleopatra.

          (FABIAN's eyes bug out. He taps DAVID on the
          shoulder.)

                    DAVID
Mark Antony is my dream role.

                    FABIAN
Mr. Amesbury, sir. There's something you should know.

BRANDY

It just so happens that we're looking for a strong actor. Rumor is you're well-equipped for the challenge.

FABIAN

Mr. Amesbury, please.

DAVID

I've been preparing for this role my whole life.

BRANDY

I recommended you to my producers.

FABIAN

MR. AMESBURY, SHE'S A SLAGHORN!

(DAVID and BRANDY finally look at FABIAN.)

FABIAN

Look!

(FABIAN shows DAVID the phone. DAVID looks up at BRANDY.)

DAVID

You're from Twerk n' Jerk Productions?

BRANDY

They're willing to cut you a deal this time, David.

DAVID

I told them I'm a classically trained actor.

BRANDY

All the better. We'll make it worth y our while. We'll even call it Julius Cisor.

DAVID

My answer is no. It's been 'no' for the past ten years.

BRANDY

They're prepared to offer you half a million dollars.

DAVID

Five hundred thousand... dollars?

FABIAN

Mr. Amesbury?

    (BRANDY walks behind the table and hovers over DAVID's left shoulder. FABIAN hovers over DAVID's right.)

BRANDY

We can make your dreams come true, Mark Antony.

FABIAN

Don't do it, Mr. Amesbury. Think about your fans.

DAVID

That's a lot of cash.

BRANDY

Think about how they'll see you in a new light.

FABIAN

You don't want that light, Mr. Amesbury. It's not right.

DAVID

I mean, porn is still acting. It's cinema after all.

BRANDY

Mark Antony and Cleopatra have a sexy love affair...

FABIAN

Cleopatra had chlamydia, Mr. Amesbury.

DAVID

It's a classic story too.

BRANDY

...Right before I let the snake bite me.

FABIAN

Remember how the Cisor drove the snakes back to Wicked Canyon, Mr. Amesbury.

DAVID

I could make this one movie and do theatre for the rest of my life.

BRANDY

Give me y our best Mark Antony line!

(DAVID stands.)

DAVID

Friends! Romans! Cunt--

(FABIAN grabs the pitchfork from BRANDY's hand and points it at her threateningly.)

FABIAN

Back off, you Slaghorn strumpet! I am Kirkaldy, Defender of the Avians, and you are trespassing on hallowed ground.

DAVID

Flügelhorn, have you lost your--

FABIAN

It's Fabian, Cisor! And this is for your own good. I can't let you do this.

(FABIAN and BRANDY circle each other).

DAVID

Hey, put that down!

(FABIAN points the pitchfork at DAVID, and DAVID's hands thrust into the air.)

FABIAN

One move, and I'll pop her chesticles.

BRANDY

Don't worry, Cisor. I can take this little dental dam.

FABIAN

I'd like to see you try.

(FABIAN lunges at BRANDY, but she dodges.)

BRANDY

What was your name? Fart-again? Rabies-Inn?

FABIAN

That's Kirkaldy to you, you giant mound of platypus poo!

(FABIAN lunges at BRANDY, and she is "stabbed.")

BRANDY

Ouch! Oh my God, I can't have any bruises, you nutcase. I'm filming a scene tomorrow.

DAVID

With me as Mark Antony.

FABIAN

Over my dead body, Cisor!

BRANDY

You know what? Screw this. We could just cast Johnny Jiggleballs as Mark Antony.

(BRANDY leaves. FABIAN is astonished.)

DAVID

Wait, Brandy. Come back. Come back, sweet Pharaoh of the Nile!

FABIAN

I did it. I saved the Cisor from the Slaghorns. It was me! I didn't even have to die this time.

DAVID

I was destined to play Mark Antony.

FABIAN

I saved your life, and now you're going to thank me, Cisor.

DAVID

I've had a lot of crazy fans, but you are by far the worst.

FABIAN

There's only one way to do it.

DAVID

I think a restraining order will suffice.

FABIAN

No. You're going to climb on the table and say it.

DAVID

Absolutely not.

FABIAN

I saved you from hepatitis. Say it!

(FABIAN points the pitchfork at DAVID.)

DAVID

Okay, Fabian.

FABIAN

That's Fa--Hey! You got it!

DAVID

I'll say it as long as you promise to leave me alone.

FABIAN

I swear on the life of every Avian who was ever slain by a Slaghorn that I will.

> DAVID

Finally.

> (DAVID climbs up on the table as FABIAN sinks to his knees).

> FABIAN

Oh my God. That's the spot.

> DAVID

I've seen too many of my Avian brethren fall.

> FABIAN

That's it.

> DAVID

All this must end.

> FABIAN

Here it comes.

> DAVID

The Slaghorns will pay for what they've done.

> FABIAN

Say it!

> DAVID

Feel the wrath of the Cisor!

> FABIAN

Yes! Yes! Ahhh! Yes!

> (FABIAN covers his crotch.)

> FABIAN

Oh no.

> DAVID

What is it, Phoebe?

FABIAN

My underoos are filled with happy-juice.

DAVID

Happy-juice?

FABIAN

It only happens when you say it. Never any other time. I need some tissues.

(FABIAN runs out.)

DAVID

I need a new agent.

(LIGHTS GO DOWN.)

VERB LIST

This list may help you think of an action verb to summarize the action intended by the line of dialogue. This list is by no means exhaustive. Feel free to add any verbs to this list you might want to include for future use if you think of any. Obviously, these verbs have many synonyms of varying intensity, so consider adding those too.

Accept	Boost	Confront
Accuse	Brag	Conjure
Admonish	Bribe	Contradict
Affirm	Broach	Convince
Aggravate	Browbeat	Corroborate
Alleviate	Build up	Criticize
Amuse	Bully	Crush
Annoy	Cajole	Dampen
Apologize	Calculate	Dare
Appease	Capitulate	Dazzle
Applaud	Caress	Defame
Appreciate	Castrate	Defile
Approve	Categorize	Deflate
Arouse	Challenge	Deflect
Attack	Cheer	Defy
Badger	Cherish	Demand
Bait	Clarify	Demean
Battle	Clown	Deny
Beg	Coax	Desecrate
Beguile	Coerce	Destroy
Belittle	Compliment	Dethrone
Berate	Condemn	Diagnose
Blame	Confide in	Direct
Bluff	Confine	Discourage
Bolster	Confirm	Disparage

Divert	Hammer	Negotiate
Dodge	Harangue	Nudge
Dote	Harrass	Nuzzle
Dream	Heal	Ogle
Electrify	Hold	One-up
Encourage	Humblebrag	Order
Enflame	Hypnotize	Overwhelm
Engage	Incite	Pacify
Enlighten	Inform	Pamper
Ensnare	Infuse	Persecute
Entertain	Ingratiate	Persuade
Entice	Insinuate	Pester
Entreat	Inspect	Placate
Entrust	Instruct	Play coy
Espouse	Interrogate	Plead
Eviscerate	Intimidate	Please
Exalt	Inveigle	Plunder
Exhort	Jeer at	Poison
Explain	Justify	Pounce on
Expose	Kindle	Praise
Flabbergast	Lecture	Preach
Flatter	Lighten	Pressure
Flaunt	Lull	Prod
Flay	Lure	Provoke
Flirt	Maneuver	Pry
Foil	Massage	Punish
Fondle	Menace	Quiz
Forgive	Mock	Reassure
Forewarn	Mollify	Rebut
Galvanize	Nag	Remind
Goad	Nail	Reminisce
Grieve	Needle	Renounce
Guide	Negate	Reprimand

Repulse	Shirk	Subdue
Rescue	Shock	Subjugate
Ridicule	Sneer at	Suffocate
Rouse	Soothe	Summon
Ruin	Speculate	
Salute	Spoil	
Savor	Stalk	
Scold	Startle	
Seduce	Steer	
Sell	String along	
Shame	Stymie	

GLOSSARY

A quick guide to definitions of the terms mentioned in the text.

action beats – the duration of a specific tactic the character will use to achieve their objective in the scene.

action verb – a word that expresses an action.

anagnorisis – a Greek term suggesting a moment of recognition for a character.

backstory – the specific part of a character's previous lived history that informs a line of dialogue or plot moment.

biography – a character's entire lived history.

beat change – the change from the tactic a character has been using to a new tactic.

callback – a reference, direct or indirect, to a previous moment or line in the story or script.

catharsis – the purging of emotion (repressed or otherwise) from both the character and the audience.

central dramatic question – a direct question that articulates a character's journey or overall conflict, usually phrased as "will character action verb object?"

character pass – a revision of the script or story focusing only on characters' actions and dialogue, usually focusing on one character at a time.

connotation – the feelings surrounding a given word; implied meanings.

denotation – the literal dictionary definition of the word.

dialogue pass – a revision focusing only on the spoken dialogue in the script or story.

direct object – the recipient of the action of a verb.

dramatic function – the purpose a character serves in a story; how they impact the plot and other characters.

expositional dialogue – dialogue with the sole purpose of explaining backstory or biography.

external superobjective – a goal over the duration of the story for a character that is tangible. The audience or reader can see the character win or lose this goal. Also known as the "want."

foreshadowing – hinting at or presaging events that are to come.

hashtag technique – a way of analyzing, then indicating the subtext of a line of dialogue when doing a dialogue or character pass.

hamartia – a character's fatal or tragic flaw, which, if not overcome will destroy the character or prevent them from achieving a goal.

internal superobjective – something internal a character must overcome in order to achieve their external superobjective. Also known as the "need."

intransitive action verb – an action verb that does not require a direct object to receive the action.

line – spoken dialogue.

need – something internal a character must overcome in order to achieve their external superobjective. Also known as the "internal superobjective."

on the nose – dialogue that expresses exactly what a character means without any subtext.

overwriting – overexplaining, exaggerating, or harping on details or story points.

pantser – a writer who writes "by the seat of their pants," without much, if any, preparation or planning.

payoff – the resolution to a line or moment set up earlier in the story or script.

peripeteia – the moment of change for a character, usually coming after a moment of recognition.

plotter – a writer who outlines or plans elements of the story before drafting. Also known as a "planner."

scene objectives – the little objectives within a scene a character must achieve on the way to achieving the superobjective.

set up – a moment or line that prepares, or "tees up," another moment or line that happens later.

stakes – what the character stands to lose if they do not achieve a goal.

subtext – a hidden meaning, implication, tone, or connotation in a line.

superobjective – a goal stretching over the duration of the story. Can be either internal or external.

theme – a universal statement or message conveyed by the story. Usually makes a statement about a topic. Can be expressed by: theme = topic + statement about topic

topic – a very general life concept or subject.

transitive action verb – an action verb that takes an object. This verb must be completed with a direct object.

treatment – a summary or synopsis of a story written in prose form.

underwriting – when details cannot be inferred or extracted from a written moment, yet the writer thinks the details are present. Forces the reader to make leaps in logic to accept character and plot details.

verb phrase – a few words grouped together that express an action and which function as a single action verb. For example, "triumph over."

want – a goal over the duration of the story for a character that is tangible. The audience or reader can see the character win or lose this goal. Also known as the "external superobjective."

ACKNOWLEDGEMENTS

My first thank you should go to my students. I am constantly inspired by your creativity, ideas, and willingness to learn. Interacting with so many of you have made me ponder and practice the application of so many strategies discussed in this book. To the best writing group in the world: Jennie Jarvis, Heather Startup, and Julie Anne Wight. Thank you for your honest notes, supportive feedback and criticism, and your constant friendship these many, many years. Every writer should have a support system like this. To my acting teachers across the years: Jackie Bartone, Jennifer Jarackas, Christy Hamilton Poggi, and the late great Yvonne Suhor. I'm sure not many actors take acting classes to become better writers, but you have made me better at both. To writing conference coordinators: Keep doing the good work. There are many writers like me who find value in the wonderfully informative sessions you provide. To my publisher, the team at Beating Windward Press: Thank you for your guidance through this process.

To my dear family and friends: Thank you for your support across many, many years as I take on creative endeavors. It means so much to me to know I have your support and love. Thank you for always being a listening ear when I need to talk, and a listening ear when I have a lame joke I want to try out.

I have to save my most biggest thank you for my husband Kevin, the most important person in my life. I love you and the life we are building together. Thank you for always being there for me and thank you for knowing that "being there" sometimes means I need quiet time to write. I am so grateful you have given me my own "happily ever after."

ABOUT THE AUTHOR

Allen Gorney is an actor, writer, and college professor. He holds a BA and MA in English (Film Analysis/Dramatic Literature Concentrations) from the University of Central Florida and has been teaching courses in literature, rhetoric, and film at the college level for several years. As an award-winning instructor, he has also earned the prestigious National Board Certification. A working actor who has worked in theater, television, commercials, and film, he received dramatic training from the American Academy of Dramatic Arts in New York and studied at Shakespeare's Globe Theatre in London. As a screenwriter, he has earned recognition and critical praise from festivals across the United States. He has also written, produced, and acted in several plays, short films, and music videos and has served as a dialogue coach on both short and feature films. His first novel *The Scottish Bitch* was published under the pen name Jameson Tabard and is also available from Beating Windward Press. He currently teaches at a media arts university in Florida.

CPSIA information can be obtained
at www.ICGtesting.com
Printed in the USA
LVHW080734051121
702404LV00005B/131